the little red schoolbook

T0346949

the little red school- book

Søren Hansen and Jesper Jensen
translated from Danish by Berit Thornberry

pinter & martin

The Little Red Schoolbook

First published in the UK in 1971 by stage 1

This original and uncensored edition, with additional material, published by Pinter & Martin 2014.

Reprinted 2018, 2022

Published in arrangement with Søren Hansen and the estate of Jesper Jensen.

ISBN 978-1-78066-130-8

Also available as ebook

Original Danish edition published by Hans Reitzels Forlag A/S, Copenhagen, title "Den lille røde bog for skoleelever"

Research and footnotes for 2014 edition by Helen Bilton

Pinter & Martin would like to thank Søren Hansen, Vibecke Aagaard, Ingrid Moore, Kevin Smith and Geraldine Homewood, as well as Richard Handyside and the original team behind the first UK publication of this book.

Based on a design by Ian Escott

Printed in the EU by Hussar Books

Contents

Publisher's introduction to the new edition

Forty-five years is a long time and much has changed in the world since this book was originally written. Many things haven't changed, however, and this is one of the reasons why we have reprinted this book exactly as it was written. This way you can see the original text, as it was intended to be read.

There are a couple of places where we have changed a word because the word in the text would not be understood now – these are marked in the footnotes. There are very few of these, however – most of what you will see was in the original. We have removed outdated contact details and addresses, and updated them where appropriate.

Wherever we think there has been a change from what the book says, we have researched more up-to-date information and then added the newer information in footnotes at the bottom of the page. We hope you will find it interesting to see what has, and has not, changed in the time since this book was first written.

The original text refers throughout to 'he' and uses words like 'headmaster'. We've left them like that so you can get a flavour of the original, but you should be aware that these days we would write with less gender-specific language, using 'headteacher' and he/she.

The book refers to several books and publications and quotes prices (in pennies!). Since the collapse of the Net Book Agreement in 1997 prices of books are not fixed so you couldn't do that any more in a similar book. Most of the publications mentioned in this book are still available second-hand though some of them are now rather expensive.

Over forty years ago, the UK publisher of *The Little Red Schoolbook* was successfully prosecuted under the Obscene Publications Act, a decision that was upheld by the Appeal Court and subsequently by the European Court of Human Rights (although 17,000 copies were already in circulation!). A second, censored edition was then published, but has long been out of print.

We hope this republication of the original text helps in a small way to draw attention to this largely forgotten book, which we feel in many ways is still very relevant today.

Foreword

When Jesper Jenson and I first published *The Little Red Schoolbook* in 1969 it was a protest against the Victorian/authoritarian school system with its robotic discipline. The book was mostly read by teachers and parents, but it was also widely enjoyed by students, from Japan in the East to Mexico in the West. To satisfy public demand it was translated into twenty languages. In Australia the government was on the brink of being overturned. The Pope condemned it as immoral. The publisher in Greece was jailed for daring to bring it to the public. The UK Authorities confiscated the book at the publisher's office. The publisher took his case to the European Court of Human Rights, but lost.

Fortunately today, the Victorian/authoritarian school is no more. More sophisticated methods to discipline and standardise children have been carefully put into place. Children have been placed into a competitive arena. Education is no longer a personal process of forming a child into an adult. Now it is examination, classification, a standardised curriculum, intellectualisation, league tables, etc. Gone are the creative subjects. It is 'Beat your buddy'. The pupils are the losers.

Unfortunately, I still believe the book is needed.

Søren Hansen, 2014

Introduction to the original British edition

This book was first published in Denmark in 1969. Since then editions have come out in Finland, Germany, Holland, Norway, Sweden and Switzerland, and American, Italian and Spanish editions are also planned. Children at school obviously face much the same sort of difficulties everywhere – although you shouldn't forget that the problems faced by children in the rich countries where this book has appeared are nothing like as serious as the problems of the millions of children in poorer countries who don't get enough to eat, let alone have an opportunity of going to school.

Conditions vary from country to country, as well as from school to school. Unlike many countries which have a single basic state education system, Britain has a very wide variety of schools, both state and private. Points of detail may differ, but the problems discussed in this book arise in all sorts of schools.

This book is meant to be a reference book. The idea is not to read it straight through, but to use the list of contents to find and read about the things you're interested in or want to know more about. Even if you're at a particularly progressive school you should find a lot of ideas in the book for improving things.

This British edition has been edited by a small group of children and teachers, with the help of many other people. We've tried to make it as useful as possible, but you can help us to make it even more useful.

Write and tell us about problems that aren't discussed in the book. Let us know if the book helps you to understand things better and to improve the situation at your school. If you're lucky enough to be at a good school, let us know how particular problems have been solved in your school.

Your ideas, suggestions and criticisms will be used to make future editions of the book more useful. If you have particular problems, we'll try to put you in touch with other people who have the same problems, so that you can try to solve them together.

Do write anyway and let us know what you think of the book. Even if you don't like it at all – write and tell us why.[1]

We hope you'll enjoy reading the book and, above all, that you'll use it.

> Alan, Elizabeth, Hilary, Richard, Roger, Ruth

---

1 The original publishers, stage 1, no longer exist, but you can get in touch with Pinter & Martin at www.pinterandmartin.com.

All grown-ups are paper tigers

Many of you think, "It's no good. We'll never get anything done. Grown-ups decide everything and our friends are either frightened or don't care."

Grown-ups do have a lot of power over you: they are real tigers. But in the long run they can never control you completely: they are paper tigers.

Tigers are frightening. But if they're made of paper they can't eat anyone. You believe too much in the power of grown-ups, and not enough in your own capabilities.

Children and grown-ups are not natural enemies. But grown-ups themselves have little real control over their lives. They often feel trapped by economic and political forces. Children suffer as a result of this. Cooperation is possible when grown-ups have realised this and have started to do something about it.

If you discuss things among yourselves and actively try to get things changed, you can achieve a lot more than you think. We hope that this book will show you some of the ways in which you can influence your own lives. We hope it will show you why grown-ups are only paper tigers.

Søren Hansen and Jesper Jensen, 1969

Education

Everybody wants to find out about things. Education should teach you how to find out about the things you need to know and give you the opportunity of developing your own particular talents and interests to the full.

The trouble is that few people really know how to do this. Those who do know, or at least have some good ideas, are not the people who actually control the education system. The system is controlled by the people who have the money, and directly or indirectly these people decide what you should be taught and how.

Whatever teachers and politicians may say, the aim of the education system in Britain is not to give you the best possible opportunity of developing your own talents.

The industries and businesses that control our economic system need a relatively small number of highly educated experts to do the brain-work, and a large number of less well educated people to do the donkey-work. Our education system is set up to churn out these two sorts of people in the right proportions – although it doesn't in fact succeed. As a result, schools in Britain just aren't able, in general, to give you a proper education. For a start they don't get enough money, and this has many results. Most schools have hopelessly inadequate buildings. Teachers don't get paid enough. There aren't enough teachers. Most classes are far too big for teachers to be able to give you proper individual attention. There aren't enough books.

Instead of helping you develop as an individual, schools have to teach you the things our economic system needs you to know. They have to teach you to obey authority rather than to question things, just as the exam system encourages you to conform, not to be an individual. And teachers and others who are against this system can't do much about it on their own.

This book can't tell you how to solve this basic problem. It does try to help you make the best of a bad system. What you get out of your education will largely decide what you get out of your whole life. So you have a right, and a duty to yourself, to insist on getting the best possible education. You should know how the present system works and what its limitations are. But you must not let this stop you demanding a proper education.

Learning

How do we learn things?

Many teachers think that they themselves should decide what you should know. They think it's a waste of time to let pupils try things out for themselves and let them discuss things.

Many teachers think that pupils should have to do boring things as well, because then they'll learn that there is something called duty and that they'll have to obey orders and do boring things later in life.

Many teachers think it's unnecessary to explain to their pupils why they must learn certain things. They just say they must because it's in the course.

These teachers are wrong. They should always explain. If something's worth learning, they should tell you why. If it's not, but they have no choice, they should tell you so honestly (see *Education*, page 18).

To learn anything demands an effort from you – and some encouragement to make the effort. School should give each individual pupil as many opportunities of learning as possible.

Remember that everything you've learnt, you've learnt yourself. You have to do the work of learning. Your teacher can't do it for you. What he can do is give you as many opportunities as you need and encourage you to get on with it yourself.

Remember too that you can only learn about things if you're allowed to think them out for yourself.

About learning

If you're bored, you learn only how to be bored. Whether the timetable says maths, geography, or whatever.

If you have to do as you're told all the time, all you learn is to be obedient and not to question things. You learn not to think.

If you're forced to learn, you learn that learning is unpleasant. It's no help that the teacher says it will come in useful later in life.

If you're not given any responsibility or allowed to choose or decide anything for yourself, you learn to be irresponsible and to depend on others, even if your work gets 10 out of 10.

If you're always taught to do things the same way, you learn only one way of doing things and it becomes harder to cope with all the new things you'll have to face later on.

To learn anything useful it's important that
- you should want to;
- that you find the subject interesting;

- that you understand why you have to learn it;
- that you get a chance to say something yourself;
- that you are allowed to work on the subject in your own way;
- that you are allowed to cooperate with your friends.

If you think a particular teacher isn't very good at teaching, you should try to work with him to make his teaching better (see *How to have influence*, page 49).

You yourself know best when you are bored. Or when you feel you're never allowed to say anything. Tell the teacher. He wants you to learn. Most teachers also want you to enjoy lessons. Because then they enjoy them more too. Talk to your teacher and see if you can't persuade him to make his teaching more interesting.

If he refuses to talk to you, try speaking to someone else in authority. You may well find that this doesn't get you anywhere. If it doesn't, and the problem is really serious, you'll have to try other measures (see *How to make a complaint*, page 60).

You have a right to good teaching. And it's you who notice best when the teaching is bad. You get bored, or you muck about.

Better teaching

This demands something from you. Maybe you think it's easier to let the teacher do most of the work in lessons. But you won't learn very much that way. And it's often boring.

There are many ways of teaching apart from just going through the work you've prepared and then setting more, or just following the book. There are many ways which are more fun. Ways in which you learn more just because the method is more varied and more enjoyable.

Lessons

What is a timetable?

Schools have to be organised. Lesson times, breaks, meals, courses, etc. all have to be fixed. If these things weren't organised, nobody would be able to get anything done at school.

But often the authorities insist on order for order's sake. Sometimes because this makes life simpler for them. Sometimes because they want to impose their own ideas of conformity – no long hair, no "crops", no mini-skirts, no maxi-skirts, no talking in the corridor, lining up in the playground etc.

To make sure you learn enough of each subject, the school draws up a timetable. This is usually decided only by the headmaster, not by the teachers and certainly not by the pupils.[2] Most school timetables cover just one week. But a six-day or ten-day timetable might be better. This would make it possible to work on one subject for longer at a time.[3]

A new school at Countesthorpe in Leicestershire is working without any fixed periods at all. The pupils are allowed to decide themselves what they want to work on in a fifth of their time. They can work at their own speed on the subjects that interest *them*.[4]

In a few schools they've changed the system of classes too. At one time perhaps a hundred pupils are brought together for a lecture, then everybody splits up into small groups for discussion.

---

2 Since this book was written even the headteacher doesn't have much discretion, and must follow the National Curriculum, which was introduced into primary schools in 1989 (www.gov.uk/government/collections/national-curriculum).

3 Many secondary schools do now have a ten-day timetable but whether this allows longer periods for studying a subject is debatable.

4 Countesthorpe Community College (www.countesthorpe.cc) no longer operates like this, but their website does promise individualised learning and a choice of 'pathways'. 'Free schools' (a type of academy school), which became possible in 2011, have potential for greater flexibility, although they are still required to abide by the National Curriculum.

Timetables can also be worked out so that pupils are divided not according to their ages but according to individual progress in each subject (but see *Streaming*, page 88).

There are many possibilities. But of course it's always easier for the authorities to carry on in the same old way.

Perhaps you're not so good at French as your friends. Maybe they only need eight lessons while you need sixteen. But according to the timetable you all get the same number of French lessons. Also, one teacher may be able to teach a particular subject much better than another.

So you shouldn't believe that it's only the number of lessons which decides whether or not you learn something.

Religious education

The only subject British schools *have* to teach, by law, is religion.[5] The Education Act of 1944 says that schools must have a minimum of one religious education lesson per week, and a religious assembly every day. But you have the

---

5   Again this is not quite the case any more; all maintained schools must follow the National Curriculum. Academies have greater freedom but are still subject to Ofsted regulation and are therefore limited in the expression of that freedom.

right to opt out of RE and assembly. Just get a note from your parents saying they don't want you to have any RE, and give the note to the teacher concerned. If you have this note you can't legally be forced to do RE.

Apart from RE, schools are free to decide what subjects they will teach. In practice this usually means that the headmaster decides, not the teachers or you.[6]

How do most teachers teach?

Most teachers use all the lessons for what's called "class teaching". Here it is the teacher who decides what is to be discussed, read or written about.

From time to time he asks you questions or tells someone to come up to the blackboard. He often asks questions not to find out your opinion about things but to find out if you're paying attention or if you've understood what he's been saying.

Some teachers believe that individual teaching means simply listening to pupils one at a time. But if the whole class has to listen too, then it's still class teaching. Perhaps they hand out a book towards the end of the lesson from which you read a short passage and then talk about it.

Perhaps they divide up the lesson so that you read, write and talk in the same lesson. Or else

6   See note 2 on page 24.

they simply check your homework and set the next lot.

This is all class teaching. It's the teacher who decides what is to be done in the lesson. If your teacher always uses this method, he's wrong. There are many other methods and he should use them.

Motivation

To make the work more interesting some teachers use slides, tape-recorders and pictures during their lessons.[7] It is of course a good idea to make the work as interesting as possible. And it's also a good idea to use things apart from just school-books. Teaching aids are a very valuable supplement to personal teaching, although they should never be used to replace personal teaching.

But these other methods are sometimes used just to persuade pupils to work on things that don't interest them at all or that will be completely useless to them after they've left school.

This is called "motivation". A better word for it might be "bait". When it's impossible to get pupils

---

7   Modern technology has vastly expanded the range of
    tools. A modern teacher is likely to use electronic media,
    the internet, audio and video alongside books and
    pictures.

interested in the subject-matter itself the teacher tries to make its outward appearance entertaining. If the subject really isn't worth learning, then this is a waste of everybody's time. In this case, try to exploit these methods to get on to other things which may have nothing to do with the subject but which interest you, and are therefore useful.

How do the minority of teachers teach?

A good teacher may sometimes let you decide yourselves whether you want to work alone, in twos or in groups. Perhaps he also lets you decide what you want to work on within the subject you're doing. He may give you a project and a few suggestions on how to tackle it – and then leave the rest to you. He may send you off somewhere to collect information. He may just throw you into the middle of a subject and let you experiment for yourselves. This can be very difficult, but you really learn something from it.

We all know that there are a few subjects in which you're allowed to decide for yourself what you're going to work on and how. These are the subjects that some teachers and many parents regard as unimportant, subjects like art, woodwork, and cookery.

If your teacher gives you a chance to get on with things yourself, help him by making use of this opportunity. Don't forget that he may himself feel uncertain about trying something new. The important thing is that he's prepared to try.

He's often afraid that you may do something for which he'll be criticised by the authorities. He may get laughed at by the other teachers for wanting to try something new with you. The other teachers are worried that the pupils may prefer him and his methods and start criticising their own old-fashioned methods.

A teacher who wants to let you try something new can also have problems with parents. Many parents think that the only teaching that's any good is the kind they had themselves. They're afraid their children won't learn enough unless it's hammered into them as it was when they went to school.

If you're lucky enough to have a teacher like this, it's a good idea to think of the difficulties he has and give him your support. In return you'll enjoy working with him. He'll almost always be easy to talk to and will give you good ideas and advice and help you with practical and personal things.

If you're bored

If you're bored in lessons, remember that the teacher may be bored with the subject too. Try to get a discussion going on something different –

and he may jump at the opportunity.

But if you really can't persuade the teacher to make his teaching less boring, then you always have possibilities of escape. You know some of these possibilities very well:

- writing notes to each other;
- drawing on the cover of books;
- playing with your ruler and rubber;
- making paper planes under the desk;
- thinking about what you're going to do after school;
- reading comics or thrillers[8] under your desk.

Escaping is understandable in these circumstances. Here are a few more suggestions on how you can escape from boring lessons:

- work out how you're going to spend your pocket-money;
- plan your spare time;
- get together with someone else who's bored and exchange notes about a film or something on TV or anything else that interests you;
- write an article or a letter to a newspaper – perhaps about that particular lesson;
- read *The Little Red Schoolbook*;

---

8 'or pornographic magazines' removed after consultation with the surviving author. See more on pornography on page 112.

- draw something in a book that looks like your exercise book; the teacher will think you're taking notes;
- write a poem on a book cover;
- write a letter you should have written long ago;
- write to us for example and describe the lesson.[9]

What is "mucking about"?

Mucking about is another form of escape. You muck about when you're bored. Mucking about is escaping from a teacher who isn't so strict that he frightens you. You often muck about if you've had a lousy time in the previous lesson, or because there are too many stupid school rules, or just because you want to let off steam. This is a natural reaction.

Many pupils muck about whenever they have a substitute teacher or a new teacher. But remember – they may seem not very good at first simply because they're unsure of themselves and haven't got to know you yet. It's best to give them a chance.

Some teachers would like to make their teaching interesting but simply don't get a chance because of all the noise you make. Never muck about unless you're absolutely certain that the teacher is an incurable bore and you've tried every way of persuading him to change.

9   See note 1 on page 16.

But remember – even if a teacher *is* a bore, mucking about won't actually solve the problem. You'll have to take more positive action (see *How to make a complaint*, page 60).

Are you allowed to do things yourselves?

Educational psychologists have shown that pupils must play an active part in lessons if teaching is to be effective. Playing an active part means that you should do or say something yourselves during the lesson. You're not playing an active part if you just sit listening all the time. And you're not playing an active part if you're bored. Try to tell your teacher this.

Altogether it's a good thing to ask the teacher straight out why he does what he does. Or ask him in writing.

How are lessons used?

When you ask your teacher questions about this he may at first answer you sharply or get angry. Ask again anyhow – but in a polite, helpful way.

But before you ask questions it's a good idea to have noted exactly how your teacher has used the last ten lessons. Try for example to keep a record of your maths lessons to see if you do anything other than first mental arithmetic, then correcting homework and checking that everybody has done it, then for the last twenty minutes going through some of the written problems in the next lesson.

If the last ten lessons have been spent in exactly the same way you have a right to ask why.

Perhaps your teacher uses the lesson for something completely different to what's laid down in the timetable. He may tell you about all sorts of different things. Maybe you can easily get him talking just by asking him some question or other. Make use of this. Start a discussion on something that interests you about school or about the teaching.

There are many jobs that have to be done at school apart from teaching itself. Teachers do some of these jobs without pay because they're genuinely interested. There are also jobs they have to do without extra pay, very much against their will, like playground duty.

If your teacher uses your lessons for other things than teaching, then you can protest. He is there to teach you, not to correct essays or write reports or read the paper.

If he's helping with the school magazine, with a play you're putting on or with the school council, it may be a different matter. Maybe there are things you can discuss with him or help him with.

Find out more

To find out more about how lessons should be used, read some of the books that teachers use when they're leaning how to teach. You may find some of these books a bit difficult to understand. So it's a good idea to get together with some friends to read them. Go to a public library and ask for a good book on, say, teaching geography. Once you've read a book like this you may be able to suggest some new ideas to a boring teacher.

There are also some very good books about experimental schools and books that discuss the whole question of what education should be about. *Summerhill*, by A. S. Neill (Penguin, 35p) gives one idea of what schools can be.[10] *Risinghill*, by Leila Berg (Penguin, 30p)[11] shows how disgracefully our education system often treats teachers who have really good new ideas. *A Letter to a teacher* (Penguin, 40p)[12] is a really good book about the problems of some Italian children – just like your problems.[13]

---

10 The original book is still available second-hand but the author also wrote a new version in 1998 *Summerhill School: A New View of Childhood* (A. S. Neill, St Martin's Press, 1998)

11 Still available second-hand.

12 By N. Rossi and T. Cole. Still available second-hand.

13 In the past 40 years there have been many more books written about education. Or you can use the internet to

Homework

Why homework?[14]

As well as organising the time you spend at school, schools also try to organise some of your free time. There isn't enough time to teach you everything during school hours so they give you work to do at home. This lowers the pressure on an overcrowded timetable.

Homework shouldn't be just a routine duty, set because it says so in the timetable. It should give you a chance to work on things on your own and develop the ideas discussed in class. It's important for you to learn to think things out for yourself and to express them clearly.

Often teachers don't realise how hard it is for you to work at home. Perhaps you have to do your homework in the room where the rest of the family is watching TV. Perhaps you do a paper round in

---

research further – for example Ken Robinson's famous TED talk www.ted.com/talks/ken_robinson_how_to_escape_education_s_death_valley

14 Homework is a much debated issue. See www.tes.co.uk/article.aspx?storycode=6319948. Several books have been written, e.g. *The Homework Myth* (Kohn, Da Capo Lifelong, 2007), *The End of Homework* (Kralovec and Buell, Beacon Press, 2001). The current president of France, François Hollande, wanted to ban homework for primary age children in 2012.

the morning or when you get back from school, and when you finally get to your homework you're exhausted. Perhaps you just have a lot of other interesting things to do in your free time.

If you find it difficult to work at home, tell your teacher about it. Get together with some friends who have the same problem and ask the school to let you stay there a bit longer each day to do your homework.

There are no laws which say how much homework you must do. You should make a fuss if you feel you're being given too much homework to do.

Most teachers – and especially most parents – just can't imagine that you can learn anything without doing homework. Tell them that in Sweden compulsory homework has been abolished.[15]

Can parents help?

Remember that your parents aren't meant to help you with your homework. As a rule parents simply aren't capable of helping you. What you're learning at school is perhaps something they can't

---

15 This may no longer be the case, but Swedish schooling (and Finnish and Danish) is often held up as an example of more progressive education than the British model. See, for example, compulsory Minecraft www. pcgamer.com/uk/2013/01/15/minecraft-becomes-a-compulsory-class-for-swedish-school.

remember any more.

And perhaps the way things are done nowadays is different from the way their teachers used to do it in the old days. So it's easy to get into an argument about it.

But if your parents *are* able to help, so much the better – as long as you tell your teacher you've had help.

If there's something you can't understand, and your parents or friends can't help, don't do your homework. Tell your teacher why.

Cheating or cooperating?

Cheating means just copying the answers from someone else or from the back of the book. Cooperating means working together with other people so that you understand things better. But some teachers call this cheating. Ask these teachers to tell you how you can cooperate without cheating.

In some subjects, like maths or physics, it's useful to have the answers so that you can check if you've got the problem right before going on to the next one. But you're not learning anything if you just copy down the answers without working them out for yourself. If you do this you're cheating – and wasting your own time.

Make your homework useful

Try to get hold of a different book to the one you're using at school, in history for example. Read about the period you're doing at school in this other book. Then ask questions from the new book. This can start a useful discussion.

Try also to read ahead in your book, then ask questions about your new homework. Ask other questions too about homework. Why can't we work in twos on the homework for tomorrow? Can I write a poem instead of an essay? Why can't pupils give talks?

Plan your work

Many teachers prepare only one lesson at a time, if they prepare at all. If they don't prepare properly, their teaching is not planned – unless they just follow the book word for word, which makes for boring lessons.

You shouldn't make the same mistake when you plan your own education. If you make a long-term plan, look things up in other books, and let yourself be inspired by the world around you, your years at school will be much more useful and you'll learn much faster. For this reason you should also ask your teacher to work out a long-term plan with you. He should tell you about the main subjects you're going to work on in the future and refer you to other books in which you can look up more information.

Teachers

Teachers are there to teach you not the things that you as an individual really need to know, but rather the things that other people think you ought to know (see *Education*, page 18).

Many teachers don't really know the practical value of the things they teach you. They've learnt about them from books and they pass this knowledge on to you, without always explaining how and why it will be useful.

Many teachers have never done anything apart from teaching. As a result they may not know much about life outside school. Many of them come from a different social background to their pupils and were brought up at a time when the world looked different. As a result they may not understand you and your ideas about the different world you are being brought up in.

All this is not the teachers' fault. They work at school every day. They are forced to prepare you for exams set by other people with which they themselves may disagree (see *Public exams*, page 177).

Things should be arranged so that each teacher, every now and then, automatically gets a year off so that he can get experience of something apart from teaching, instead of getting stale and out of touch with the world outside school. At the moment, if a teacher ever does get a year free he usually has to go back to "school", yet again, and sit and learn from more books. Much of his knowledge won't be any use to you, but he won't get a chance to find out about many things which would be useful to you.

The teacher's duties

Teachers get paid a fixed amount, regardless of how much teaching they actually do. They are meant to get a certain number of hours free for preparation and marking. But they're often asked to give up some of these "free periods" to teach or to do other things, without getting any extra pay. They get paid the same amount however few "free periods" they actually get and however many hours of their own time they use for preparation.

Some teachers spend a lot of their own time preparing. Others don't prepare at all, not even in their "free periods" at school. But remember that if a teacher spends all his own time preparing, he won't be a complete human being. He'll become just a teaching machine.

It's very difficult to say exactly how much a particular teacher gets paid. The exact amount depends on how many years he's been teaching and what training he's had. He gets extra allowances if he's head of a department or has some other position with extra responsibility. But most teachers are underpaid in comparison with people in other jobs who have the same level of training.

Some teachers go on courses in their holidays, without always getting paid more as a result, even if it makes them better teachers.

Apart from extra duties connected with teaching itself, there are many other jobs that a teacher does more or less voluntarily and without extra pay. He sells savings stamps, organises visits to the theatre or trips abroad, goes to meetings with other teachers, arranges the school dance, etc.

In the last few years teachers have become discontented about all these extra jobs and are already starting to say "no". For instance, after a long campaign teachers are now no longer obliged to do a dinner duty. But since it's very rare that adequate alternative arrangements have been made, some teachers feel that they have to go on doing it, even though they really need a break and some time to prepare. Support your teachers in these campaigns.

In the end it will benefit you when they don't have to work all hours. A teacher who's exhausted by far too many hours of work can't do anything very well. Most teachers in Britain are overworked if they do

41

the job properly, and it's particularly exhausting if they're new to the job.[16]

What have teachers been taught?

Most teachers have received their knowledge about children, society and the world through education. Few teachers have done other jobs before they qualified and began to teach. They have gone to school, taken their exams and gone on to teachers' training college or university.

Teachers who qualified before 1970 may only have a university degree without any actual teacher training. Now new teachers have to have some teacher training. A normal training college course takes three years. A university degree course followed by teacher training takes four or five years.[17]

Most secondary school teachers have learnt to teach one particular subject and know most about this

---

16 This whole section is just as true now as 40 years ago. Teachers do now have compulsory 'PPA' (Preparation, Planning and Assessment) out of the classroom, which is a couple of hours a week for which the school provides cover. In practice, as the text says, this is often eroded.

17 All teacher training now involves a university degree. Students can either do a BEd and then go straight into teaching or do any degree and then either a PGCE or directly into on-the-job training.

subject. They may have been to courses later to learn more. It's by no means certain that they will be allowed to teach the subjects they like and know most about. It's hard to find people to teach certain subjects, so many young teachers have to put up with teaching subjects they don't like.

Much of what teachers are taught at college is purely academic knowledge. They do learn a bit of theory about children, but it's only when they start teaching that they really get a chance to test this theory. So you can be fairly certain that young teachers straight from college won't know much about how to plan teaching.

Many teachers tend to blame other people when things go wrong. They invent theories about the youth of today being particularly difficult, or they blame it on bad working conditions, or on the headmaster, or on the parents.

They may be right (see *Education*, page 18). But they may just be making excuses for their own failings. In either case they won't feel particularly happy about the situation. It could encourage them to try to change things if you try to understand their difficulties and discuss possible solutions with them.

What do teachers know about you?

Even if over the years your teachers spend many

hours with you, the chances are they won't know much about you. Your parents may know a bit more, and your friends will know most.

But you should realise that the school does have a lot of information about you. For example the results of medical or psychological examinations, your exam results and teachers' reports. This information is treated as confidential, but it's available to teachers, police and child welfare authorities.

As a rule an ordinary teacher doesn't know
- what your living conditions are like;
- where your father and mother work and how much they earn;
- how many brothers and sisters you have and where they go to school;
- how your parents get on together;
- what your parents think of the teacher and the school;
- what you do in your free time;
- whether you like the teacher and the school;
- whether you have a lot of interests outside school;
- whether you do a paper round or another job;
- how much time you spend on your homework.

A bad relationship often develops between teachers and pupils because they don't know enough about one another. If you feel that a teacher is treating you badly because he doesn't know enough about you, don't feel afraid of telling him more about yourself, who you are and what you want to do.

Relationships between teachers

Relationships between grown-ups are in many ways similar to relationships between children. They may hate one another or they may be good friends. They often get together in groups that quarrel among themselves.

Most teachers try to hide this from children and pretend they all agree. They say this is to avoid confusing pupils or making them doubt what's right. This may be true. But it's often because they're afraid of not having enough knowledge and authority to stand up for a particular point of view (which in most cases is probably right). Many teachers are afraid of losing their job or not getting promoted. For this reason they don't dare speak out if they disagree with the headmaster or the head of their department. So it's rare for a teacher to dare to tell his pupils what he really thinks about conditions at the school.

Most schools operate in a sort of pyramid. At the top there's the headmaster. Then the heads of department. Then ordinary teachers. And at the bottom, the pupils. The decisions are made at the top of the pyramid and passed down to the bottom.

It would be much better if everybody in a school could exchange their ideas freely and have a real say in the way things are done. Policy should be decided democratically. As a start, try to get your own teachers to express their ideas to you and allow you to do the same. And make sure at the very least that there's a school council (see *About representation*, page 211). Use it to get things changed.

What happens at staff meetings?

Teachers talk about many things at staff meetings – things to do with the school, things to do with themselves, things to do with you. The meetings are often long and boring, and for the individual teacher many of the things discussed are rather trivial.

Many staff meetings are not real discussions. The headmaster or some other senior teacher tells the teachers what he wants them to do. The teachers who are after promotion say how much they agree. The other teachers just keep quiet because they know there's no point in trying to say anything different.

Staff meetings are closed to pupils, and it's rare for approaches or queries from pupils to get discussed. But it's easy for you to get some idea of what's been discussed. See if there's any change in the teachers' behaviour just after a staff meeting. And note whether new subjects are brought up for discussion in class. If this happens, it's because the teachers have talked about it at the meeting. Ask your teacher to tell you what's happened.

Pupils' behaviour in the playground and corridors is often discussed at staff meetings. The school authorities are interested in seeing that the rules are obeyed. After a meeting you'll often notice that some of the teachers are a lot more keen on keeping you out of the corridors, making you keep the playground tidy, etc. You'll know then that these things have been discussed at the staff meeting and that it's been agreed to make an effort.

Don't worry. It won't be long before the teachers have forgotten what they decided or were told to do at the staff meeting. It's difficult for them anyway to make sure that all the school rules and regulations are obeyed – and besides many of them would much rather not have to.

It doesn't follow that all teachers have agreed with everything that's been decided at a staff meeting. Even if there's an open disagreement at the meeting, it's usually the headmaster who makes the final decision, and all the teachers then have to accept it whether they agree or not.

Teachers are dogs on leads too

There shouldn't really be any conflict between teachers and pupils. Teachers do have a lot of power, but even they are forced to do a lot of things which they may not want to do.

Teachers don't have any say in what they're taught at training college. They have very little say in what they teach you: their teaching has to be geared to the exams you have to take (see *Exams and tests*, page 175).

They can exert their power over you during their lessons, but they don't have much say in the general way the school is run. They can make you pick up every scrap of paper on the classroom floor, but they can't do much about the conditions they work in themselves. There are still schools where teachers don't have a common-room for themselves. There are some schools where the teachers have to go outside the school premises if they want to have a pee.[18]

And the authorities expect teachers to be particularly "respectable citizens". They're not expected to get drunk in public or to have open affairs with other teachers' husbands or wives. It's frowned on if they don't turn up at assembly in the mornings – even if they don't believe in religion. And they're usually expected to conform to certain

---

18 It's highly unlikely that this is still the case now, but conditions for teachers in many schools are by no means comfortable.

standards of dress – usually the headmaster's standards. In most schools this means that male teachers are always expected to wear a jacket and tie. In many schools women teachers still aren't allowed to wear trousers if they want to.[19]

When it comes down to it, teachers have remarkably little control over their own lives – if they want to remain teachers, that is.

How to have influence

Teachers often influence you without you noticing it. Directly or indirectly they put across certain standards of behaviour which may be good or bad. They control your development to some extent – but this doesn't mean that you can't have any control over it yourself. The relationship between children and grown-ups can only be right when both sides influence each other.

Don't think that it's impossible to influence a teacher. Even if you may not notice it at the time, everything you say and, especially, everything you do will influence your teacher.

To have influence it's important to remember
- That it's easier to influence someone if you like them and they like you.

---

19 Women teachers these days can wear trousers in most schools. Ofsted do involve themselves, however, in teachers' standards of dress.

- That the most influential thing you can do is to be honest (and tactful).
- That you need to know the person you want to influence – and to understand why he does what he does.
- That a person who's frightened is hard to influence: he often gets angry so as to hide his fear.
- That it's best to bring disagreements out into the open if everybody knows they exist.
- That discussing and sorting out disagreements is a good way of learning more about each other. It also helps clear the air.
- That if words fail, you can try positive action.

If you like a teacher

Liking a teacher doesn't mean that you always agree with what he says and does. Maybe he takes life a bit too easy because he likes teaching your class and has become lazy.

Don't be afraid of telling a teacher you like that you enjoy his lessons. But at the same time try to influence him to make things better.

A teacher who gives you a great deal of freedom and who is honest with you can have problems with older, more old-fashioned teachers. He's usually the one who speaks up on your behalf in the staff common-room, perhaps without telling you anything about it.

So be careful not to get him into trouble by talking about him to teachers you don't really like. Defend him if you think he's being attacked. Always show loyalty towards those you think are loyal to you.

Honesty is influence

If everybody dared to be honest with each other all the time, our present school system would collapse very rapidly. But as a rule neither teachers nor pupils dare to be honest with each other.

Neither teachers nor pupils usually dare to say that they're bored. And even if a teacher knows this, he can't usually face up to it and deal with it. So you should realise that if you speak the truth to a teacher in one way or another, he will be influenced, even if he doesn't show it at the time.

Truth can be told in many ways. Don't be afraid to tell a teacher about your own attitudes, about what you like, who your friends are, and what sort of problems you have outside school hours.

Use the school magazine, the school council, discussions in class, to talk about subjects which you find important. Try to arrange to do an English essay on how you see the school, and use it to write about the most important things, the things you really want to express.

If you want to call a teacher by his first name, just start doing so and carry on doing so until it has become a habit for all of you. Remember that one side – the teacher – probably does it already.

Action is influence

If being honest doesn't work and all your suggestions get talked to death, then act to show that you mean what you say. Actions speak a lot louder than words.

The best way to act is to simply do what you've talked about for so long. If there are things you've wanted to introduce into school – whether in lessons, in breaks or after school – and you've been refused, start them by yourselves.

Showing that you are united can be enough to start things moving and get the changes made.

If you're not given the sex education you think you have a right to, start using the notice board in your classroom to provide this education.

If you don't like sitting looking at the back of each other's necks, try moving the desks or tables round yourselves.

If you think the classroom is dull, start making it more attractive and interesting – put up posters or notices on the board.

If stronger action is called for, see *Demonstrations*

and strikes, page 56.

Teachers and their authority

Most bad and authoritarian teachers are tied up in knots or afraid of something or other. They're often afraid of their pupils and think they have to appear strict and unapproachable. They're afraid that the pupils may be right and that they may be wrong. They're afraid that there'll be chaos if they give up their power and authority.

This fear arises because they don't believe in other people's ability to organise themselves and find their own solutions to problems. This lack of faith in others may be due to a lack of belief in themselves. They're insecure and have to rely on their authority all the time.

If you want to influence your teacher you must know something about him. Ask other teachers if you don't dare to ask him yourself. Find out, for instance, if he likes the other teachers. If he doesn't seem to like teaching you, ask him why. Find out about his good and bad points, and try to encourage the good rather than attacking the bad.

It's difficult to influence someone who's afraid

If your teacher is frightened of you and therefore afraid of doing anything new with you, he's usually very hard to influence. In order to influence each other, it's necessary to feel reasonably secure. So to influence a frightened teacher, make him feel secure. Show him you're willing to cooperate. Give him a real chance to explain what he's trying to do. If you ask to do new things, explain that this is not in order to test him out, but so that everybody can be freer and therefore enjoy themselves more. Once he realises that in some situations things can be done in a different and freer way than he has known so far, it may be possible to make some progress.

Teachers who are afraid that things will get chaotic if they take off their masks, their false authority, won't usually go further than allowing something new "just for once" or "as an experiment". Make use of this opportunity. If the "experiment" works, the teacher should obviously be willing to do it again.

Disagreements

If things can't be sorted out through discussion and cooperation, and if everything about which there's real disagreement just gets talked to death, it may become necessary to use direct action as another form of influence.

Disagreements and conflicts of interest don't only arise between teachers and pupils. They also arise between different groups of pupils, and between groups of teachers. Both among pupils and among teachers, there will always be some people who are content with things the way they are and who therefore disagree with those who want things changed.

Disagreements are not bad in themselves. They only become bad if they're not sorted out. If a disagreement gets sorted out, everybody learns from it.

In the last section we suggested some methods of bringing disagreements out into the open and sorting them out. It may prove impossible to get the two sides to be honest and start solving the problem. You may have made your point about wanting to stay in the classroom during break, but when discussion gets going properly people opt out and won't stand up for what they've agreed they want. They opt out either because they're afraid or because they can't be bothered.

Even if it takes a long time and a lot of talking, you really must try to get everybody united behind you. Get the issues discussed in the school council, if there is one. If there isn't a school council, the first step must be to get one set up. Meanwhile, use the school magazine, discussions in the playground, etc. to get more people behind you.

Perhaps all the suggestions made by the school council are either rejected by the authorities or accepted but not acted on. Repeat the suggestions, several times, and insist on action. Use all available channels (See *How to make a complaint*, page 60).

If everything else fails, it may be necessary to take other steps such as demonstrations or strikes. You should be aware, though, that this is the most drastic method of all, and you should be prepared to get punished. On the other hand, the more of you there are behind a demonstration, the smaller the punishment and the better the prospect of success will be.

Demonstrations and strikes

There are many things to remember if a demonstration or strike is to have any chance of success.

You should first make sure that there are a lot of other pupils who are dissatisfied with the same thing as you – and preferably some teachers too.

You should have tried every other method first to get your grievance settled.

Before you start, everybody should be told about the problem and what you want to achieve. Use the school magazine and notice boards. Make your case clear by using posters, banners and slogans. Talk to teachers who have your confidence. Talk to other pupils during breaks.

Try to explain the problem to your parents, but

don't count on getting their support. You should be prepared for the worst. You should be prepared to get punished. You should be prepared for newspapers sometimes distorting the facts and being against you.

You should be prepared for some of your friends to give in when parents or teachers threaten punishment.

The demonstration itself

A demonstration doesn't have to be a walk-out. The form of the demonstration should be suited to what you want to achieve.

If, for example, you don't want to have to line up in the playground, demonstrate by just going straight into the classrooms.

If you want a soft drinks stall, start by selling drinks yourselves.

If you want to stay in the classroom during breaks, demonstrate by not going out when the bell rings. Just sit down in a group.

If you object to having the school magazine read by the headmaster or a teacher before it appears, print it and distribute it illegally.

If you're dissatisfied with a certain teacher and he refuses to talk to you, organise a strike. Get everybody to stay in the playground during his lessons all day.

Get leaflets printed or duplicated to explain what you want. If it's an issue of general educational policy, like corporal punishment or overcrowded classes, get in touch with pupils at other schools. Try to form a real pupils' union. In France in 1968 the pupils' union did organise a large-scale strike and succeeded in getting important changes made.

There is in fact already a small but growing pupils' union in Britain. It's called the *Schools Action Union*,[20] and their programme calls for proper democracy in schools and for making schools real centres of education rather than industrial training centres. Get in touch with them and find out where their nearest branch is and what it's doing.

Whatever you do, don't be put off by being threatened or spoken to angrily.

After the demonstration

If anyone is singled out for having started the demonstration, be loyal to them. Go with them if they are to be told off or punished.

Check that promises you are given during the

---

20 This, and the similar 'National Union of School Students', was short-lived. Students' unions are common in universities and colleges, but the only cross-institutional one is the NUS (National Union of Students) of which there is no equivalent for primary or secondary students.

demonstration are kept after it. Don't believe that things will necessarily get solved just by being left to staff meetings or the school council.

If you have no other way of expressing your views, send letters about the problem to the editors of newspapers and magazines. Try making your own "wall newspaper": put up a big sheet of paper on a wall in the playground or some other suitable place. Write up your own views, then everybody else can add their opinions and write about their problems too. This "newspaper" may get torn down – but not before a lot of people have had a chance to see it. And it's easy to put another sheet of paper up.

Usually a demonstration or strike will make the authorities and teachers more frank with you, whether it's actually successful or not.

Welcome teachers who want to discuss *The Little Red Schoolbook* with you, even if they try to talk you out of what you want. Do discuss it, but prepare for the discussion by talking about things among yourselves beforehand. Then you'll be able to make your points too.

But remember: people should be judged by what they do, not by what they say. This applies to both teachers and pupils.

How to make a complaint

First and foremost, there must be a good reason for complaining. It's a serious matter for a teacher to be complained about. But you shouldn't be deterred from complaining because you're afraid, or because you can't get your parents to support you. Schools and teachers are like other institutions and people: if they're never criticised, they'll never get any better.

Collect evidence

You must first collect evidence. This means getting examples of the things you think the teacher does badly or wrongly. Maybe he persecutes one of your classmates. Maybe he lets you go too early, or lets you off his lessons because he can't keep you all in order. Maybe he beats you illegally or does other things he's not allowed to do (see *Punishment: what is allowed?* page 67).

Get your friends to help you put things down on paper. You must put your evidence in writing or nobody will believe you. It's best if several of you do it. Don't forget to include the time and date in each case.

Go to the teacher or to the school council

Once you've collected evidence for, say, a month, first show a copy of it to the teacher and talk to him about it. Most teachers would prefer to keep this sort of thing within the class, so maybe you can settle it by talking to the teacher concerned.

If talking doesn't help, submit the complaint to the school council for discussion. If this doesn't produce any results, submit it in writing to the headmaster or the school governors. Always keep a copy.

If you want to complain about a teacher hitting pupils you don't have to wait until you've collected evidence of several cases. Nor do you have to go to the teacher first. You should go straight to the headmaster.

Go to the headmaster

If there's no school council, or if a letter from the school council doesn't help, you should go to the headmaster yourselves. But it's a great help if your parents know about it beforehand. Try to get their support. If several pupils suffer from the teacher's treatment, it's best if several parents complain. It's enough if they just sign the complaint. They don't have to go to the headmaster with you. You must get your friends to sign the complaint as well – as many of them as possible. The headmaster will almost certainly promise to talk to the teacher concerned. Try to find out if he actually does. If he doesn't, complain to him again.

A complaint to the headmaster or other authorities should always be in writing, and should be signed. And there must be examples of what you're complaining about.

It can be difficult to write this sort of letter and make a list of examples. Get some older friends or grown-ups to help you. See *Example of a complaint*, page 64, for a basic outline of a letter of complaint. Don't lose your original notes and the detailed examples. You may need them again later.

Go to the authorities

If complaining to the headmaster doesn't help, try complaining to the parent-teacher association, if there is one for your school. This body has no power to make decisions, but if they support your complaint they may be able to put pressure on the headmaster to do something about it.

If this doesn't work either, try going to the school governors. You're not officially meant to approach them, and you may have to do a bit of research to find out who they are.[21] But it's obviously worth trying.

Before approaching the school governors it's important to get the support of your parents. You

---

21 Not any more. Schools will often have details of governors and how to contact them on their websites, or office staff will help you.

should get them to sign the complaint as well as your classmates. The headmaster is likely to support the teacher, and as a rule the authorities will support the headmaster. So the evidence must be good and as many people as possible should sign the complaint.

If there are good grounds for your complaint and it's got this far, the chances are that something will be done about it. If nothing is done about it, there are several things you can do.

You can collect new evidence and complain again.

You can send the complaint to the Local Education Authority.[22]

If you can't be bothered to deal with the authorities or feel it won't get you anywhere, you can go to the press. Write a letter to the editor of the local paper or get in touch with a journalist. Newspapers are usually very interested in writing about cases like yours. The local BBC office or your local radio station might also be interested. But be sure that you can prove what you say, or you can get into serious trouble. Also make sure the papers don't distort your case.

Trade unions can also exert a lot of pressure, and are likely to be sympathetic and try to help if

---

22 And/or Ofsted.

approached in the right way. Try to find someone who's an active member of a union, or ring the *Trades Union Congress*[23] and ask them for the address of the local Trades Council.

Another organisation that may be able to help is *The National Council for Civil Liberties.*[24] They have recently launched a campaign on children's rights, and will certainly be willing to give you any help they can themselves, as well as suggesting other organisations that may be able to help.

Example of a complaint

To the Headmaster/Headmistress, ...

School (or To the Board of Governors),

The undersigned wish to complain about Mr/Mrs/ Miss (teacher's name) who teaches (subject) to our class (name your class).

We think it wrong that (and then a short description of what the complaint is).

To explain our point of view, we have made a list of examples of the kind of thing the teacher does and which we think is wrong. (Then give your evidence. First write the date and time, then a description of what the teacher did, whether there was any reason for it, who suffered as a result, and

---

23 www.tuc.org.uk 020 7636 4030
24 Now Liberty: www.liberty-human-rights.org.uk

anything else that's relevant. It's best to be brief. The most important thing is that it should be easy to understand what you think is wrong. After this list of details you should finish with something like this:)

We have talked to the teacher concerned about this, but we don't think it's been any use. We therefore ask the Headmaster (or the Board of Governors) to look into this complaint and see that something is done. We would be grateful if you could let us know what is being done as a result of our complaint.

Yours sincerely, …………………………………

Don't forget
You must only complain if you can prove your complaint. This means you must have evidence. If you have the evidence, don't be put off from complaining because you're afraid or because it's too difficult. It's always difficult to improve things, but it pays in the long run.

Can a teacher be sacked?

It's quite difficult to get a permanent teacher sacked. But younger teachers are often employed on some kind of temporary basis. This makes it easier for the authorities to sack them or at least transfer them to another school.

This often means that a teacher who has a "revolutionary" approach to teaching can easily be sacked. But it may be impossible to get rid of a really bad, long-established teacher.

If there are problems with a teacher, the school will almost always support him, even if everybody can see that something's wrong. So it can be very hard to get a complaint or suggestion for improvement accepted and acted on. Try anyway.

If a teacher is so bad that nobody in the class gets any benefit at all from his lessons, then do complain about him. Complain several times if necessary.

The actual grounds on which teachers can be suspended or dismissed aren't usually specified in Local Education Authority regulations. If a teacher has epilepsy or certified mental illness or tuberculosis his appointment is automatically terminated. In these cases he can only be appointed again after a certain period free from the illness concerned. Apart from this, teachers can be suspended for fraud or "other grave offences".

The authorities don't specify what a "grave offence" is. This means that different headmasters, boards of governors and LEAs can have completely different ideas of what offences are "grave". Being sentenced to prison is usually, although not automatically, considered sufficient reason for dismissal. Other reasons depend initially on the headmaster. In most schools the authorities would consider something like hitting a pupil round the head a much less "grave" offence than a teacher going to bed with one of his or her pupils.

Relatively few teachers actually get dismissed, for whatever reason. Instead, they are "encouraged" to resign. This amounts to the same thing, but it isn't so "nasty".

Remember that even though the regulations may not allow the dismissal of a bad teacher on the grounds that he teaches badly, the authorities, if they agree with you, may be able to persuade him to resign.

Punishment: what is allowed?

The best way of teaching is to use encouragement and rewards, not punishments. Psychologists discovered this a long time ago. But not all teachers and parents have discovered it yet. There are many kinds of punishment. There's caning, detention, telling off, ridicule and sending people out of the class. Some punishments are allowed in school. Others are forbidden. For example, it's forbidden for teachers to take things away from you and keep them. If a teacher has confiscated something of yours he has to give it back. (This applies to *The Little Red Schoolbook* too!)

Overcrowded classes, inadequate buildings, etc. (see *Education*, page 18) often make it difficult, if not impossible, for teachers to keep calm and use the "right" methods all the time. Remember, if you treat your teachers as human beings, most of them will respond.

Some punishments are not called punishments but are, all the same. A teacher may dislike one or several pupils. He may "pick on" them by ignoring them or dealing with their work in an unpleasant way. He may give them worse marks than they deserve. You can stop a teacher punishing you in this sort of way (see *How to make a complaint*, page 60).

School rules

Almost all schools have rules. Pupils should participate in making the school rules. Have you helped make the rules in your school?

Most school rules say what pupils must and must not do. They rarely say what teachers are allowed to do. The rest of this section tells you something about what teachers can do.

Corporal punishment

There is no actual law governing the use of corporal punishment in schools.[25] The only

---

25 Corporal punishment was in fact banned by law in

national regulation comes in a Department of Education and Science memorandum (no. 531, 10 May 1956). This says that all schools must record corporal punishment in a Punishment Book, which has to be kept for three years and is open to inspection by the ministry.

Under British common law, teachers are regarded as being *in loco parentis* to children in their charge. This means that teachers have the rights and duties of "a normal, prudent" parent. Parents, and hence teachers, are legally entitled to physically punish a child who misbehaves. They only break the law if the punishment is improper or excessive. There is no established definition of what "improper or excessive" actually means. As a result, it's very rare for a teacher (even rarer for a parent) to actually get taken to court for excessive punishment.

Even if a teacher does get taken to court, the school authorities will usually support him. And the courts themselves often tend to have a distinctly old-fashioned view of what is excessive. They tend to be lenient with the teacher, unless the punishment has been really outrageous.

Courts also tend to use a rather wide definition

<hr>

state schools in 1987 and in private schools from 1999. Therefore the rest of this section no longer applies, except that teachers are still considered *in loco parentis*.

of how far a teacher's authority stretches. Courts have supported teachers who punished pupils for fighting on the way to school and for smoking on the way home.

Regulation of the use of corporal punishment in schools is left to Local Education Authorities. Some LEAs lay down who is allowed to use corporal punishment (maybe only the headmaster) and even specify the maximum length and thickness of canes (although these regulations are often disregarded). Other Authorities have only very vague regulations, or leave it entirely up to the individual headmasters. Even if one accepts the use of corporal punishment in schools, the wide variations between different LEAs make the present system totally unjust.

Should it be abolished?[26]

Corporal punishment in schools is obsolete and should be abolished. It's been abolished in British prisons and in the army and navy. It's been abolished in schools in most other Western countries. Why is it still used in most British schools?

Part of the answer is that most parents and teachers still support the use of corporal punishment, both in school and out. It was used when they were

---

26 Again, it has been abolished so this section is now out of date.

children and they still think "a short, sharp lesson" is the best answer to any misbehaviour. In this respect, they treat children as they would treat a dog which "misbehaved" on the carpet.

Quite a lot of research has been done on the use and effects of corporal punishment in schools – although far from enough. Time and time again it's been shown that corporal punishment can do serious harm to disturbed, backward or mentally handicapped[27] children. Yet it's most frequently used on precisely these children. These unfortunate children often show their distress in "abnormal" or "delinquent" behaviour. What they want is more attention and encouragement. What they get is a slap or a caning. This can make them even more disturbed and backward – and it isn't even effective in stopping their "abnormal" behaviour.

Corporal punishment isn't effective on ordinary children either. If a teacher gives you a cuff round the ear (often quite unjustifiably) it doesn't make you change your attitude and really pay attention: it just makes you resentful. If you get called to the headmaster's room for a caning you may be a bit afraid and it will hurt for a while. But it doesn't miraculously make you "see the light" and

---

27 The terms 'backward' and 'mentally handicapped' are not used now; you are more likely to hear of 'children with learning disabilities'.

transform you into a "nicely behaved little boy". At best it'll make you try not to get caught again. And when it's over, the chances are you'll treat the whole thing as a big joke.

But it can have more serious effects. In many schools, working-class children resent the middle-class attitudes of the teachers. They feel the school wants them to "talk posh" and to adopt middle-class standards of behaviour that are foreign to them. They respond by refusing to cooperate with the teachers or actually "misbehaving". Instead of trying to understand them and talk to them, the school tries to beat it out of them, literally. This just makes the children more resentful, more difficult to communicate with. And it widens the gap between "them" and "us".

When teachers and parents say "well, I got thrashed when I misbehaved at school" it often seems almost as if they want to "get their own back" by having you thrashed as well. They need to go back to school and study the facts. Psychologists have shown that corporal punishment can do serious harm to disturbed children. Other experts – and plain common sense – have shown that it isn't effective on children, ordinary or otherwise.

Even an official government report (the Plowden Report on primary schools) has stated that corporal punishment is "ineffective in precisely those cases in which its use is most hotly defended" and "it should be banned". But most schools in Britain go on using corporal punishment.

Don't despair. Some parents and teachers are against corporal punishment, and more and more organisations are starting to campaign against it. In particular there's an organisation called *STOPP: Society of Teachers Opposed to Physical Punishment.*[28] They're still only a small minority and there's a lot of ignorance and lazy thinking to be fought before they win. But corporal punishment will eventually be banned in Britain.

A special note

In many so-called public schools (see *Independent schools*, page 184) not only teachers are allowed to use the cane. Senior pupils, prefects or head boys are made responsible for keeping discipline and are allowed to beat other pupils with a cane or with a slipper.[29] This barbaric practice was quite accurately portrayed in a recent film called *If.*[30]

---

28 This organisation is no longer in existence. There are currently campaigns to abolish spanking (by parents) altogether.

29 All forms of corporal punishment are now banned in independent schools, so prefects are no longer allowed to beat up juniors.

30 Obviously no longer recent, but still available on DVD.

A prefect in a public school often has a lot of power, and if he happens to dislike a junior pupil he can easily "have him" on any one of a mass of trivial school rules (some not even written) and beat him for it. And do it again the following week. Of course he's meant to report the beating to the housemaster. But he can easily invent some "serious offence" that the pupil's meant to have committed. And quite a few housemasters don't seem to care much what their prefects do anyway, as long as they keep the place quiet and tidy.

Luckily only 10 percent[31] of British children are educated in public schools. But it's still a disgrace that children should be authorised and even encouraged to beat other children.

What else can teachers do?

If a teacher thinks you've misbehaved, there are various things he can do. He can move you to somewhere else in the room, he can make you stand in the corner or outside in the corridor. He can give you extra work to do, or give you lines, i.e. turn you into a parrot with a pen, writing out 100 times "I must not throw paper darts in class" or whatever. He can put you in detention, so that

31 Currently 6.5 percent of UK schoolchildren are educated privately and 18 percent of 16+.

you have to stay in during the dinner break or after lessons end.

Some schools have a system of marks for behaviour, as well as marks for your work. If you break a school rule or misbehave in some way, the teacher gives you a black mark or a "misconduct point". Sometimes you get a beating or some other punishment if you get too many of these black marks in a certain period.[32]

If none of these minor punishments stop you doing what the teacher considers wrong, or if you do something more serious, like smashing a window deliberately or hitting a teacher, you may get beaten, either by the teacher or by the headmaster.[33]

If you do something even more serious, or if you maybe refuse to be beaten, or if the school finally decides it can't cope with you any more (which is usually a failing on the part of the school) you may get suspended or expelled[34] from school. If you're at a private school, you can be expelled and

---

32 Not any more.
33 Not any more.
34 Usually called 'excluded' these days. A 'suspension' is a fixed-period exclusion and 'expulsion' is a permanent exclusion. Schools have ways of excluding people on 'health and safety' grounds which do not show up in their statistics.

that's that. And the same applies at a state school if you're over the school leaving age (at present 15, but due to go up to 16 in 1972/1973).[35]

But if you're under the school leaving age, it's difficult for a state school to expel you unless you've actually committed a crime and been taken to court. The school can suspend you for a limited period. But the Local Education Authority must, by law, provide you with full-time school education. So even if a furious headmaster tells you you're expelled and sends you packing, the LEA will eventually be obliged either to find another school for you or to send you back to the one you were "expelled" from.

What can you do yourself?

If you get punished for something you know is wrong, that's fair enough. If you get a minor punishment for something somebody else did, it's probably not worth bothering about, as long as it doesn't happen frequently.

But if a teacher hits you brutally, or keeps picking on you, complain (see *How to make a complaint*, page 60). If you're given a major punishment, such as a lot of extra work or a caning, for something you didn't do, or for

---

35 School leaving age has been 16 for 40 years, but as of 2013 it went up to 17 and will go up again to 18 in 2015.

something you genuinely didn't know was forbidden, refuse to accept the punishment. Be prepared to take your case to a higher authority or to the press if necessary. Don't let yourself be intimidated by any threats if you're in the right.

Demand your rights, but be polite

If you have good teachers you won't need all this information. Do remember that teachers may make mistakes without realising it themselves. Always try talking to them about it first. It's not necessary to complain every time. It's best if you can avoid having to complain.

But you shouldn't put up with continued bad or unfair treatment, You're told often enough about your duties. Remember that you have rights too.

Pupils

Your friends and schoolmates

A few facts

At school there are all kinds of people.

- Some are your friends, others you hate.
- Some you don't care for, others you'd like to know better.
- Some you look down on, others you admire.
- Some are outsiders and usually alone, others are popular and sought after.
- Some are good at everything or almost everything, others are good at nothing or very little.
- Some you can trust, others lie and rarely keep promises.
- Some are always willing to help, others are only concerned with themselves.
- Some always have good ideas, others rarely do.
- Some have ideas but can't put them into practice, others rarely have ideas of their own but are very good at putting other people's ideas into practice.
- Some can always say the right thing at the right time, others only know afterwards what they should have said at the time.
- Some are allowed to do anything, others have very strict and limiting parents.

- Some look odd because of their clothes, others are always dressed smartly.
- Some are "peculiar" because they're cross-eyed, need strong glasses or stutter, others are good-looking and have everything, from the right chest measurements to beautiful hair and fine noses.

Do you know?

- Do you know that teachers influence you and that their influence affects your judgement of your schoolmates?
- Do you know that your view of your schoolmates is strongly affected, in lots of ways, by grown-ups' views?
- Do you know that you're affected by your friends, particularly those you spend a lot of time with?
- Do you know that you are strongly influenced by things like advertising, books, comics, films, pop groups and TV?
- Do you know that in other parts of the world different standards are used for judging whether something or someone is good or bad, right or wrong?
- Do you know that the standards by which people are judged in school are not necessarily the same as those used outside school?

- Do you know that the standards by which you judge your schoolmates gradually alter as part of your personal development?
- Do you know that with a bit of thought you can work out your own system of values by which to judge both yourself and your schoolmates?
- Do you know that you can reject the standards and values which grown-ups try to force on you?
- Do you know that teachers and other grown-ups can use their system of values as a means of power?
- Don't blindly accept the values of grown-ups. Think things out for yourself and base your judgement on what you really believe.

Remember

- You are a person in your own right. In the end you're accountable only to yourself for your own actions.
- You don't have to play the part given you by your teachers and parents. You've got ideas of your own and usually know what you want.
- You know something.
- You don't know everything.
- You're as good as anybody else.
- You're not perfect.
- You can learn something from others and others can learn from you.

Working together

You're a lot stronger if you're united – whether for something or against it. But groups don't always work properly. There are several reasons for this.

Some people – real leaders – are always more active and decisive than others. But some people – bad leaders – always say more than others and listen less. Some are forever giving orders and bullying others "under" them. Some are on top, others are at the bottom. Groups like this are organised like a pyramid.

Groups don't have to work like this. There are many ways of organising things. You can create democratic cooperation, so that everybody feels that he belongs and has a real influence in all the group's decisions.

This means that you're not limited to a particular role, that you can at times lead or be led, according to the situation. It often means that you have different leaders for different things.

A group needn't have just one leader at a time. Several members of the group can lead together. This is called collective leadership. It's worth knowing that two kinds of leaders often emerge. There are those who want to decide everything themselves. They use their power to give themselves the jobs they want and they try to dominate when decisions are taken. And there are those who don't try to decide everything themselves but give others real responsibility and use everybody's energies and talents to the full.

Leaders remain leaders only as long as you let them. This is so whether your leader is a schoolmate or a teacher. He remains leader only as long as you go on obeying his orders. If you're not satisfied with your leader, choose another.

If a group decision has really been reached democratically, you should stick to it even if you disagree. You may be right to disagree and what happens as a result of the group's decision may prove you right. But if you let the others down it will be easy for the authorities to break your unity. Never let them use differences between you (i.e. age, sex, class, race, etc.) to divide you. If you think the majority decision is wrong, try again and again to convince the others, but never break the group's unity.

Be yourself

The way you behave in school may be completely different to the way you behave outside school. You may cover up your real personality. Maybe you sit "nicely" and quietly in class, looking alive and attentive – even though your real self is fast asleep.

Maybe you smoke pot or go to bed with your boyfriend or girlfriend – and don't tell your parents or teachers, either because you don't dare to or just because you want to keep it secret.

Don't feel ashamed or guilty about doing things you really want to do and think are right just because your parents or teachers might disapprove. A lot of these things will be more important to you later in life than the things that are "approved of".

Be yourself.

Intelligence

People used to think that children who couldn't manage at school were stupid. It was also believed that babies were born with a particular level of intelligence, and that nothing could be done to change this level. Neither of these things is true, but there are still a lot of people who believe them.

It's obvious that everybody's not the same at birth. But the differences at birth are not nearly as big as they become later. A strange thing happens: children who find learning difficult don't get *more* teaching at school, they get *less*. People say these children "can't cope with school" – instead of saying that school can't cope with them.

Many people disagree with this. They think that school is the one place where an effort should be made to cope with all children, including those who find learning difficult.

Intelligence can change

It's been shown that the sort of intelligence which is measured by intelligence tests can change. This sort of intelligence is often called "intelligence quotient" or IQ. The right conditions can improve a person's IQ.

If twins who are identical at birth are brought up in different surroundings, their IQs will become different. The twin who is brought up in an interesting and lively home acquires a higher IQ than the twin who is brought up in a dull, boring home where his IQ is not stimulated.

People have also made studies of children's homes. Good children's homes where children got proper care and attention were compared with bad homes where children were just left to themselves. The children from the good homes acquired higher IQs than children in the bad homes who started off on exactly the same level.

If a child can't cope at school it's wrong to say that he's stupid. It may be that he hasn't had the right opportunities, or that not enough effort has been made to teach him anything. Perhaps more time should be spent on him than on the other children.

But there are some differences

A school should be able to take into account many

sorts of differences between children – for example, how quickly they learn. Someone who learns slowly is capable of learning just as much and just as well as someone else who learns fast. But it's difficult to allow for this because there are so many pupils in each class and because there is so much to do – and maybe because the teacher doesn't know how to tackle the problem. This is where the difficulties lie.

There may be other differences. Some arise because the school only concerns itself with certain things. The school is a world on its own, and people who can't manage the particular things which the school demands often manage very well outside school once they've left.

Nobody is bad at everything. There's always one thing you can do better than other things.

What a teacher expects of you

Do you know that what you learn and how quickly you learn it is very much influenced by what the teacher expects you to learn?

Do you know that teachers think middle class pupils who are well-behaved and score well on IQ tests will learn more, and that they therefore teach them more?

Do you know that most teachers expect pupils with

working-class accents or immigrant backgrounds to learn less, and that they therefore teach them less?

Do you know that when teachers are given false information about their pupils they are fooled? In a recent experiment in New York, teachers were told that one group of pupils were very bright and that another group were not very bright. The first group enjoyed their lessons and learnt a lot, the second group had less fun and learnt a lot less. But in fact both groups of pupils were an equal mixture of all kinds of minds and abilities. What they got out of their lessons was determined not by their ability but by what the teachers expected of them.[36]

Don't let a teacher make assumptions about you and your abilities.

What does "backward" mean?[37]

Some children are so slow at learning that it's very difficult to give them the attention they need in ordinary classes. They are therefore put into special classes (called remedial classes) or into

---

36 This is Rosenthal and Rubin's 1968 Pygmalion study. More follow-up work has been done since – see www. education.com/reference/article/teacher-expectations

37 As mentioned in note 27 the terms 'backward', 'retarded' and 'mentally handicapped' have gone out of use. You now hear of 'children with learning disabilities' and 'children' with special needs'.

special schools.[38] These children are not "mentally handicapped". They are called "backward" or "retarded" Backward children manage quite well for themselves later in life. If they get enough individual help and encouragement they can learn as much as anybody else.

Being mentally handicapped usually means something quite different. Mentally handicapped children have brain damage or some illness. They find it terribly difficult to learn things and a great deal of work is needed to help them. Most mentally handicapped children can't manage on their own later in life. They often have to live in institutions for the rest of their lives.

Stupid or clever

If your teacher starts talking about who's stupid and who's clever, ask him what he means by intelligence. You'll find that he means the ability to cope with the demands *he* thinks school should make on you.

Fortunately there are many other, different demands in life than the ones made at school. People are good at different things. It's nonsense to call somebody dumb or stupid.

---

38 SEN (special educational needs) provision is now commonplace in British schools.

Streaming

Streaming is a form of rationing. Schools don't get enough money, so there aren't enough teachers and suitable buildings and equipment. The authorities think that the most efficient way of using scarce teachers is to put only pupils of a similar ability in each group or class – i.e. to stream them. Streaming is used both in primary and secondary schools.

Streaming works as a form of social discrimination. A study of British schools showed that there were 11 percent more middle-class pupils in upper streams and 26 percent fewer in lower streams than might be expected from the actual numbers in the schools. In grammar schools, the A streams were 91 percent middle-class, while the D streams were 80 percent working-class. Even in comprehensive schools the upper streams were 41 percent middle-class and the lower streams 90 percent working-class.[39]

This doesn't happen because the authorities actually decide to divide pupils up according to their backgrounds. It happens because schools only recognise essentially academic abilities – the ability to read, write, count, etc. Ability in other things

---

39 More recent studies have shown the same results. *Beachside Comprehensive* (Ball, CUP, 1981) covers streaming, for example.

such as sport, acting, dancing, etc. may be noted by the school, but ability in these things doesn't influence streaming.

Psychologists have shown that the most important years in a child's development are between 2 and 5 – i.e. the years *before* school. What happens during these years influences the rest of the child's life, both in school and afterwards. A child who gets the opportunity of exploring and developing his own curiosity and particular talents during these early years will be able to make full use of the opportunities for learning that school will give him. A child who doesn't get proper opportunities and encouragement before he starts school is unlikely to ever catch up.

Nursery schools and other forms of preschool "education" such as playgroups are not provided free for everybody[40] (see *The British school system*, page 182). The nurseries and playgroups that do exist are a rather chaotic mixture of charities and other private organisations, together with council nurseries for which parents usually have to pay fees. There aren't nearly enough places for every child anyway.

---

40 All 3 and 4-year-olds who have not started school now receive 15 hours per week of free preschool education. Some 2-year-olds are also eligible and there are plans to consider making this universal.

As a result, many children get no formal preschool "education". Some are lucky enough to have parents who encourage them to start reading, etc. But many parents don't have either the time or the patience or even the knowledge to help their children start learning: as a result, these children *start* school at a disadvantage. Their lack of what the school calls "ability" means they get put into the lower streams.

Studies have shown that children from large families or poor home conditions are most likely to be put into the lower streams. Their real potential or ability to learn is likely to be just as high as other children's, but they haven't had the opportunity of developing their potential into an ability which the school can recognise. They really need especially good teaching to make up for an unstimulating home background. Instead, they get put into the lower streams, where the chances are that the teaching will be worse or less effective (see *What a teacher expects of you*, page 85).

How streaming works

Once a pupil is in a lower stream, it's difficult to get out again. His teachers expect less of him, so he learns less, and his progress drops far behind that of pupils in the high streams. A study quoted in the Plowden Report on primary education estimated that if a streaming system was working properly 10 percent of children would normally get transferred up or down each year. But in British schools with 2 streams the average transfer rate was only 2 percent, and in schools with 3 streams the average was only 6 percent.

Children start school somewhere around their 5th birthday. Exactly when they start depends on exactly when their birthday falls in the year. What this means in practice is that some children get 9 terms at infant school (or its equivalent) while others get only 6 terms.[41] This is reflected in streaming – even though it obviously has nothing to do with a pupil's ability or potential.

Studies have shown that the lower the stream is, the lower the average age of the pupils in it is and the higher the proportion of pupils who had only 6 terms at infant school.

Streaming perpetuates and increases class differences. Working-class children start life with exactly the same potential as middle-class children. But because their home background can't offer them proper opportunities to develop their

---

41 This is no longer the case. Children are not legally obliged to attend full-time school until the term after they turn 5 (which for summer-born babies would be Year 1). However, most children start Reception (Early Years Foundation Stage) in the September that they are 4.

potential, many working-class children start school at a disadvantage. Their academic ability seems lower, so schools put them in lower streams. Some schools try to disguise their streams, but nobody is fooled by this.

Pupils put in lower streams resent it, and don't try so hard. Teachers expect less of them, so they learn less. School life seems petty and restrictive, and the school never really manages to get them interested in learning anything. As a result these pupils leave school as soon as they're 15[42] – only to find that society has nothing to offer them except "unskilled manual labour" (see *Careers advice*, page 196). They start school at a disadvantage and finish ten years later in the same position or worse.

Can streaming be changed?

Many people are seriously concerned about the bad effects of streaming. Some schools have done away with streaming altogether: academically, their results are much the same as those of streamed schools – and the unstreamed pupils don't suffer all the bad effects of streaming which we have mentioned.

But most British schools still use some form of streaming.[43] Official studies and circulars have

---

42 17 now.
43 They still do now, although many schools now stream on a per subject basis rather than across the board. So a

suggested that other methods might be better, but there will have to be a basic change in the attitudes of most Local Education Authorities before things will really change.

Meanwhile you may be able to do something about streaming in your school. Start a working group on it (see *If you haven't got a school council*, page 215). If you can get the question discussed at all levels in the school this may persuade the school to at least make the system operate more fairly, even if they won't drop it altogether.

And don't accept the ideas behind streaming yourselves. People's abilities and characters aren't shown by what stream they're in. You are equal to your schoolmates, and vice-versa, whatever stream you or they are in.

Your free time

Parents, teachers and other grown-ups often seem to be afraid of you. Afraid of the way you are, the way you behave. Afraid of the way you dress and, particularly, afraid of what you do when they can't see you.

They say they're afraid for your sake. They say they don't want to see you end up in trouble or not get anywhere in life.

---

child could find themselves in the top stream for maths but bottom stream for English.

They may be genuinely concerned for your welfare. But sometimes what they really mean by "ending up in trouble" or "not getting anywhere in life" is that you will decide to live your life differently to them.

They're afraid that you may not earn more than they do themselves. They'd rather that the work you did was a bit "better" than theirs. They'd like you to do the things they haven't managed to do themselves.

It's natural and right for parents to want a better life for their children. What's not right is for them to try to force your life into a pattern that fits their own ideas of ambition and status. This can make it very difficult for you to be yourself and lead the life you want to lead.

What does society do for you

Our society provides various places for your spare-time activities, such as youth clubs and other associations, adventure centres, etc. Some private organisations and individuals also arrange activities for you, such as guide and scout groups, dancing classes, sports clubs, etc.

Do realise that when people organise things for you it often means that they want to control you. They have plans for you. They have something they want you to do.

Youth clubs usually try to encourage you to have "good leisure interests".

Scout troops want to put you in uniform and control your associations with the other sex[44]. They aim to make you into what they call "good citizens". By "good citizens" they mean people who do as they're told and don't "make trouble" for the authorities.

Dancing classes aim to give you "good deportment". That is to say, they try to get you to behave in such a way that grown-ups will think you're "nice young people".

Sports clubs aim to teach you that what is important is to be the fastest, the strongest, and always to beat other people. And to keep your mouth shut when you lose.

When grown-ups organise spare-time activities for you, they usually have some adults around to make sure that everything happens in what they call "an orderly fashion".

One sort of activity where things happen in a particularly "orderly" fashion is junior military training in its various forms. Some schools have a Combined Cadet Force afternoon every week – it's

---

44 Girls have been able to enrol as Beavers/Cubs/Scouts since 1991. Boys, however, cannot enrol as Rainbows/Brownies/Guides in the Girl Guiding movement.

even compulsory in some places. Outside schools, there are the Army Cadet Force, the Army Training Corps and the Sea Cadet Corps. Altogether there are about 140,000 boys in these organisations.

They are meant to teach young people "good military virtues" and hopefully encourage some to join the armed forces when they leave school. Like toy guns and soldiers, war films and so many other things in our society, these organisations reinforce the idea that war is at least necessary, if not actually a good thing. Nobody seems to remember that wars haven't accomplished anything in the past except killing millions of people, most of them young people.

What can you do yourselves?

You may be able to get a corner of the grown-ups' society to yourselves if you go about it in the right way.

Form a group of pupils from your school or class. Give the group a name. Draw up some rules and aims for the group. For example: "The aim of the .... Group is to encourage friendship between pupils in the 3rd year. To do this, the Group will hold meetings twice a week. At the meetings there will be talks, discussions, pop sessions, films and other forms of entertainment." (Ask a friendly teacher how you can get hold of films and equipment.)

Once you've worked out what you want to do, see if you can't use some part of the school buildings for your meetings. Ask your form teacher or head of house or, if necessary, the headmaster. Some schools have a youth tutor whose job is to arrange precisely this sort of thing. Ask the youth tutor if your school has one.[45]

If what you want to do involves a lot of people, it's a good idea to discuss it in the school council – if there is one – and get the council to ask for permission.

Most local councils employ youth officers or youth leaders.[46] Their job is to coordinate activities and opportunities for young people. Their horizons are often limited to already existing council or voluntary organisations and clubs, but a good youth leader may be able to help you get something started yourselves.

Local Education Authorities are also obliged to provide various sorts of part-time and evening

---

45 You are unlikely to find a 'youth tutor' these days, but you will find people who are responsible for the 'pastoral' (i.e. non-academic) care of pupils. Often this is the Head of Year or the Head of Key Stage (KS3 is years 7-9 and KS4 is years 10-11).

46 Search for 'youth services' and the name of your town or city. In some areas the youth service goes by the name of 'Connexions'.

courses and classes for young people and anyone else who wants to use them. Some of these classes are for the same sort of subjects you have at school. But there may also be things like, for example, guitar-making, folk-singing, pottery and car repairing. In many areas the LEA will provide a teacher for any subject which a group of 10 people or more wants to study in evening classes. You and your friends may be able to make use of this.[47]

Remember that you can always use the press. All papers, national and local, are interested in stories about children and young people. They particularly like writing about young people who have new ideas and want to put them into practice. Ring or write to a journalist. Try the BBC and local radio too. A bit of publicity can often get things moving. But make sure the publicity is accurate.

Get your own hall

The best thing would be if you could get your own hall which you could decorate and arrange the way you wanted it. Many schools are too small, but a

---

47 Your local library will be able to provide you with details of classes in your local area. If you're searching on the internet try using the term 'adult education' – even though the classes are often open to young people too they use the name 'adult' to distinguish it from children's schooling.

bigger school *might* have a room or cellar which is empty or could be cleared for you to use.

In some places groups of young people have been lucky and managed to get halls by going to the local council. In many places the council owns buildings which are to be demolished and redeveloped sometime in the future. Try to find a building like this, then ask the council if you can use it till it has to come down.

You may be able to find a disused church hall – or even a disused church. Find out which church or organisation owns the place and ask if you can use it. Even if the hall is very shabby, it's a lot better than nothing – and you could probably rustle up some paint from somewhere and have a great time decorating.

If you can't find anywhere at all, or at least nowhere that you can call "your own" – send a letter to the mayor about it.[48] Call the letter "an open letter from young people to the mayor". Get as many signatures as you can, and get some grown-ups to sign as well. Send copies to every member of the local council, one to your local MP and one to the local paper.

---

48 Or the leader of the local council (who may not be known as the mayor). The details will be on the council's website.

Other possibilities

If you can't get anything started yourselves, of if there aren't enough of you to make it worthwhile, try any existing group or club in the area that looks interesting. Not all young people's clubs are run by grown-ups who want to keep an eye on you. There may be a local club that's just what you want. If you try one and it's no good, you can always walk out.

Sex

This section says nothing about love and very little about feelings. It gives some practical information which you may find useful. There are still a lot of schools where pupils don't get this information, where they get it too late, or where they get only inadequate or misleading information.

People go to bed with one another for many reasons.

- They are close friends and enjoy talking to one another – with their bodies as well.
- They do it because people need sexual satisfaction, and masturbation is no longer considered to be enough.
- They may lack security and seek it through sex.
- They may be under pressure to do it because everybody else in their group boasts about their "conquests".
- They may use sex as a way of exploring their own identity.
- They may have deep feelings for each other and perhaps want to have children.

Whatever the reasons may be, and however many people you may go to bed with, it will have consequences for each person.

Sex may or may not involve strong feelings. Strong feelings may or may not involve sex.

The only way to avoid unforseen consequences in sexual relationships is for both people to be honest with one another about what they are looking for.

Someone seeking security rarely finds it with someone who only wants sexual satisfaction. Someone who feels under pressure to have a sexual relationship may not find sexual satisfaction.

People who warn you against both strong feelings and sex are as a rule afraid of both. They haven't dared to do very much themselves, so they don't know enough about it. Or their own experiences of sex may have been bad. Judge for yourself, from your experiences.

Masturbation

The usual word for a boy's sexual organ is cock or prick. The usual word for a girl's sexual organ is pussy or cunt. Many grown-ups don't like these words because they say they're "rude". They prefer words like penis and vagina.

When boys get sexually excited, their prick goes stiff. This is called having an erection or "getting a hard on". If a boy rubs his stiff prick it starts feeling good and this leads to what is called orgasm. This is called masturbation or wanking. Girls masturbate by rubbing their clitoris (see below), and this may lead to an orgasm too.

Some girls, and a very few boys, don't masturbate. This is quite normal. It's also normal to do it. Some do it several times a day, some several times a week, some more rarely. Grown-ups do it too. If anybody tells you it's harmful to masturbate, they're lying. If anybody tells you you mustn't do it too much, they're lying too, because you can't do it too much. Ask them how often you ought to do it. They'll usually shut up then.

Orgasm

Having an orgasm is usually called coming.

When a boy's prick is excited enough, he eventually comes. Fluid or sperm spurts out of his prick and he knows then that he has reached the height of his pleasure. A boy's body only starts producing sperm when he reaches the age of puberty: this is usually sometime between the ages of 11 and 15 but it's not at all abnormal for it to be earlier or later.

Coming is less obvious for a girl. The feeling is different for each girl. It can be intense pleasure or excitement or a feeling of relief. Some girls come a lot faster than others. It may take some experience for a girl to find out what coming really is for her.

Intercourse and petting

When a boy puts his stiff prick into a girl's vagina and moves it around this is called having intercourse or making love or sleeping together (even if they don't sleep at all). The usual word for intercourse is fucking.

A boy and a girl can "make love" and give each other pleasure without necessarily fucking. If you don't want to fuck, perhaps because you're afraid of having children, you can find lots of other ways of giving and having pleasure – for instance by kissing and cuddling, petting or masturbating each other.

A boy and a girl can give one another more pleasure by touching or caressing each other in the right places and in the right way. Each person enjoys being touched in different places. They should talk about it and tell each other what they really enjoy.

It's easier for boys to come than for girls. A boy only needs to have his prick stroked by the girl.

For girls it's a little harder. Their most sensitive spot is a little ridge in the upper part of the vaginal lip, where it starts under the hair. This ridge is called the clitoris.

When a boy strokes it gently it goes hard (like the boy's prick, in miniature) and starts to feel good.

This may lead to the girl coming – but it may be a little time before this happens (see *Orgasm*, page 103).

Many other parts of the body are also sensitive to touch, both in boys and girls; breasts, throat, neck, earlobes, insides of the thighs, and of course the sexual organs and the area around them. These can all be caressed with the fingers, the lips and the tongue.

Contraceptives[49]

If a boy and a girl fuck, they may have children. To avoid this, contraceptives are used. Boys use condoms,[50] which are sometimes called sheaths or skins. These are covers made of thin rubber which are rolled over the prick when it's stiff. You can get them at a chemist's or from machines[51] in some public lavatories, or you can write for them to shops which advertise in papers and magazines.[52]

---

49 There are currently 15 types of contraception in the UK, the most relevant of which are discussed below. For more information see the websites mentioned on page 127.

50 Changed from 'Durex' in the original, a brand name.

51 Changed from 'automats' in the original text.

52 Today they are sold not only in chemists, but also in supermarkets and local shops. You can get them free from contraception and sexual health clinics, young people's services, and some GP practices. You can also buy female condoms though these are less widely available.

Only buy the best quality – they should always be electronically tested.

Girls use a diaphragm (or Dutch cap), the coil[53] or the pill.[54] You must have a prescription from a doctor to get the pill. The doctor will need information about your menstrual cycle (see below); but if he starts asking questions which are none of his business or starts preaching morals, go to another doctor. Female doctors are often more sympathetic.

Both boys and girls can get not only the actual contraceptives but also advice about the best methods to use from Family Planning Clinics and Brook centres. These places are often more relaxed and helpful, so you may find them easier to approach than a chemist or doctor. Look in the telephone directory to see if there's one in your area. Or contact their main office and ask where the nearest clinic is. (Addresses on page 127.)

The Consumer Association's magazine *Which?* publishes a very useful survey of every sort of contraceptive. All the contraceptives are thoroughly tested, and the survey shows which ones are most reliable and cheapest. The survey

---

53 Changed from 'loop' in the original text.
54 Hormonal contraception like the pill now comes in other forms such as implants, injections, patches and a vaginal ring.

costs £1, but you should be able to consult it in any good public library. Just ask for it at the counter.[55]

If you want to try your own doctor first, remember that his professional code requires him to respect your confidence. Even if he refuses to prescribe any contraceptives for you, he has no right to tell your parents or anybody else unless you're under 16 (the "age of consent").[56]

A diaphragm is a rubber disc with a thick edge. The instruction leaflet will say how it should be inserted – but the doctor should always tell you anyway. A diaphragm must fit properly. The doctor puts rubber rings into the vagina to find the right size. Some people think diaphragms are uncomfortable, but they don't hurt.

The diaphragm has to be put in before intercourse and whenever there is the possibility of intercourse. Remember to use spermicidal cream with it. (This is special cream which destroys the sperm. It comes with the diaphragm if the doctor gives you

---

55 This *Which?* report isn't produced any more but there is plenty of information on the internet. Use the websites of the organisations listed on page 127.
56 Since the Gillick case in 1985 doctors have been able to provide contraceptive advice and treatment to people under 16 without parental consent in certain circumstances as long as they follow the 'Fraser Guidelines'.

a prescription.) It's wise to be prepared, even if the preparations turn out to be unnecessary.

When girls haven't had intercourse before there's usually a thin film of skin at the opening to their vagina. It's called the hymen or maidenhead. This has to be removed before a diaphragm can be put in. This can happen during intercourse, or the doctor can remove it, or you can break it yourself by using a couple of clean fingers. It may bleed a little, but it hardly ever hurts if it's done gently.

The coil (or inter-uterine device, IUD) is inserted even higher up in the vagina, and you can't see it or feel it. Many doctors will only give it to a girl if she's already had a baby. The coil is left in position (unless the girl wants to have a baby, in which case she goes back to the doctor to have it taken out). It's very practical.

The pill has to be taken every day except during the time of menstruation. It must be prescribed by a doctor.[57] Don't try to get pills from somebody else, because particular types may not suit you. There are many types to choose from.[58] Some doctors refuse to give the pill to very young girls – even though they may be just as mature sexually

57 Or you can get it from a family planning/contraception clinic.
58 The two main types of pill are the 'Combined Pill' and the 'Progesterone-only Pill'. (Also see note 54 on p106).

as other girls several years older. There's usually at least one condition – that you should have had regular periods for at least a year.

Luckily the other contraceptive methods are almost as safe. If for example the boy uses a condom[59] and the girl uses a diaphragm there's virtually no risk of the girl getting pregnant. It's sensible for a girl to have some condoms in case the boy hasn't got any.

There ought to be one or several contraceptive machines in every school. If your school refuses to install one, get together with some friends and start your own contraceptive shop. The items don't take up much room, and if you order a lot at once you can usually get them cheaper (see the adverts in newspapers). But do remember, they must be electronically tested. Some are of very poor quality and hence not safe.

Ask the other person what sort of contraceptive he or she is using before you have intercourse. Don't lie about it, and try to make sure the other person is telling the truth. It's stupid to

---

59 Condoms which have been thoroughly tested will have either the British Kitemark symbol or the European CE symbol or both. The FPA recommends looking for the Kitemark. Durex, for example (a well known and widely available condom brand) have the Kitemark and the CE symbol plus their own rigorous safety testing.

risk having unwanted children. Don't think just because you've been lucky before that it'll never happen to you.[60, 61]

Wet dreams

Boys can have orgasms while they're asleep at night. This is called having wet dreams. Many boys have them. They're quite normal.

Menstruation

When girls are old enough they start having periods or menstruating. Blood comes out of their vagina, roughly once a month. Some girls start having periods (sometimes referred to as "the curse") when they are quite young. Others start menstruating later. Both are completely normal.

When girls have a period they have to use sanitary towels or tampons[62] to absorb the

---

60 'Barrier' methods of contraception i.e. condoms protect you not just from unwanted pregnancy, but also from STIs (see page 120).

61 Another form of contraception you may hear about is emergency contraception intended for after having unprotected sex or if your contraception has failed (sometimes called the 'Morning-After Pill/MAP'). There are various types available at GPs, family planning clinics and at the chemist's (although you will have to pay at the chemist's). For more information see the FPA website (www.fpa.org.uk).

62 Changed from 'Tampax' in the original, which is a brand name.

blood.[63] (Tampons are small rolls of absorbent material which are put into the vagina.) Ask your mother about this. She'll almost certainly help. Or you can talk to a friend or your older sister, if you have one.

Child-molesters or "dirty old men"[64]

In the old days people used to talk about "dirty old men". Children were told they were dangerous. This is very rarely true. They're just men who have nobody to sleep with.

There are often stories in the papers about them. They're often called exhibitionists or child-molesters. If it says in the paper that a man "behaved indecently", it means he opened his trousers and showed someone his prick. If it says he behaved with "gross indecency", it means he masturbated or got the child to touch his prick. He may have touched the child's sexual organs too.

---

63 These days you can also get more environmentally-friendly products such as menstrual cups or sponges.

64 Since this book was written in 1970 there have been many scandals involving the uncovering of sexual molestation of children and we have come to a much greater understanding of the terrible effects of such acts. Paedophiles are often known to the child (rather than a strange 'dirty old man') and we know that they are indeed dangerous. Despite the media hype though, it is still rare. If you are worried speak to your parents or teachers or call a helpline such as Childline (0800 1111).

Sometimes these incidents are followed by rape (forced intercourse), or violence, or murder. The latter is very rare, and it's usually because the man has got scared. If you see or meet a man like this, don't panic. Go and tell your teachers or your parents about it.

Pornography

Magazines, pictures and books[65] which are produced purely to excite people sexually are called pornography or porn. Porn is used in many different ways. Some people just read it or look at the pictures, others masturbate while they're reading. Sometimes porn is used with another person, for instance in marriages where sexual drive is lacking (see *Impotence*, page 114) or when the partners want a bit of variation.

Pornographic pictures are usually of people in the nude (mostly girls), having intercourse or caressing each other. But there are other kinds – for example pictures of intercourse with animals or pictures of people hurting each other in various ways. Pornographic stories describe the same sort of thing.

---

65 The internet is nowadays a major means for people to access porn. When this book was written it was more difficult to get hold of porn, which was then mainly in the form of magazines and videos.

In Britain some pornography, called "hard-core pornography", is banned.[66] But in some countries, like Denmark, there are no restrictions.[67]

Sexual appetites vary a lot. Some people want to see pictures or read about things that they would never actually do themselves. But it's possible that some desires which may be harmful to other people may be satisfied harmlessly through pornography.

Anyway it's a fact that the amount of "criminal indecency" in Denmark has dropped sharply since pornography became legal there.[68]

Almost all pornography gives a false idea of reality. It describes men who are able to make love for hours on end and have several orgasms within a short period. There are also stories about girls who want to make love all the time and in all kinds of different ways.

---

66 These days some hard-core pornography is not illegal (though it is restricted), but so called 'extreme' pornography, which includes child pornography, is banned.

67 Denmark made child pornography illegal in 1980.

68 Studies did show this, but there appears to be no conclusive evidence yet on the effect of legalisation or prohibition of pornography.

Porn is a harmless pleasure[69] if it isn't taken seriously and believed to be real life. Anybody who mistakes it for reality will be greatly disappointed.

But it's quite possible that you may get some good ideas from it and you may find something which looks interesting and that you haven't tried before.

Impotence

Some men find it difficult to have an erection. This is called being impotent. Impotence is caused by many different things. It may just be because the man is nervous or very tired, in which case it probably won't last long.

Temporary impotence is quite common. If it does last, the man may need advice or help from a doctor.

Homosexuality

Everybody is different – in sexual matters too. Some people are only attracted towards the opposite sex; some are attracted towards their own sex; some are attracted towards both sexes. People attracted to both sexes are called bisexual. People attracted to their own sex are called homosexual or queer

---

69 Today many people have concerns about the exploitation of people involved in being pictured or filmed for pornographic purposes. Other concerns include the objectification of women, and the issues around a whole generation of young people growing up believing that what they see in pornography is normal sex.

or gay.[70] At least 10 percent (i.e. one in 10)[71] of the male population has homosexual tendencies. For women the percentage may be a bit lower.

In purely physical terms, homosexuals make love just like anybody else, although of course they can't have intercourse in quite the same way. Their love and their feelings are just as real and genuine and natural as anybody else's.

Many of them have great difficulties because in our Christian culture they are considered sick, abnormal or even criminal. In many other cultures homosexuality is recognised just like other forms of sexuality.

Homosexuality has recently been made legal in Britain, but only "between consenting males over 21, in private".[72] However homosexuals are still often persecuted by ignorant people. (Female homosexuality, which is called lesbianism, has *never* been illegal in Britain.)

---

70 Also lesbian. The term 'queer' is considered by some people to be offensive.

71 This statistic probably comes from the Kinsey reports (Kinsey, A. 1948 and 1953) which are no longer considered necessarily valid. The latest Integrated Household Survey by the ONS says that 1.5 percent of UK adults identify as gay, lesbian or bisexual.

72 The age of consent was lowered to 18 in 1994 and 16 in 2001.

Many homosexuals live together in stable relationships. The time will come when homosexual marriages are recognised.[73]

There are many other forms of family life apart from marriage between one man and one woman. People can have group marriages or live together in a group as a commune. But in law our society still only recognises one kind of family – marriage between one man and one woman.[74]

There are several organisations which can help homosexuals and other people who are "different" sexually. The Albany Trust provides a counselling and referral service: this means that homosexuals and others can go there to talk to someone about any sexual problems they may have, and get referred to other organisations or individuals who may be able to help further.

The Gay Liberation Front[75] is a new and very militant organisation which campaigns for an end to every sort of discrimination against

---

73 Gay marriage became legal in the UK on 29 March 2014.

74 See note 71 on page 115. Civil partnerships have been legal since 2004.

75 The GLF does not exist in this form any more. Other organisations which do campaigning work are Stonewall (www.stonewall.org.uk) and the Pride movement.

homosexuals and bisexuals. The Student Advisory Service[76] offers sympathetic help and advice to young people on all sorts of problems, including sexual ones. Kenric is a London social club for lesbians. The addresses of all these organisations are listed at the very end of this section.

Normal and abnormal

It's normal to be different. We all are.

People use the word "abnormal" to mean many things. They may mean something which doesn't fit in with their particular standards (for example regarding school or religion). They may mean something which goes against the traditional view of what is right and wrong. They may simply mean something of which they themselves are afraid.

"Abnormal" is a very dangerous word. It's often used as an excuse for the persecution and repression of some people by others. It's particularly misused in the sexual context.

It's not considered abnormal for people to have red hair or collect coins or play the bagpipes. So why should it be considered abnormal for some

---

76 Now non-existent. Colleges and school have advisory services you can access or any of the organisations mentioned (such as Stonewall) have information and advice.

people to fall in love with others of their own sex, to like unusual positions for intercourse or to like being caressed in an unusual way.

If you're not allowed to enjoy special interests which don't harm anybody else, it's usually because of other people's intolerance. You may feel that you're the only person who experiences things in a "strange" way, and you may think you are abnormal. It can be a help to discover that there are many other people who are almost the same as you. There always are.

Find out more

If you want to know more, ask some grown-ups in whom you have confidence. But don't take everything they say as gospel truth. Many grown-ups are afraid to talk about sex. And many of them don't know much about it.

You may find some useful books in your local library. But remember, there are many bad books about sex. A recent pamphlet analysed 42 so-called "sex education" books and found that *only* one of these books could be really recommended as a source of accurate, reliable and helpful information for young people who want to know about sex. The pamphlet is called "Sex Education: the Erroneous Zone" and it's well worth reading just for the hilariously funny howlers they've found in sex books, quite apart from being valuable as a source of information. (The National Secular Society 28p).[77]

The two books they particularly recommend are *Boys and sex* by W. B. Pomeroy[78] (Penguin 20p) and *An ABZ of love* by S. and I. Hegeler[79] (New English Library 55p). The second book is not strictly speaking a sex education book, but it has good illustrations and is full of the frank, useful information you need.

All these books ought to be in your school library for everybody to read – but they probably won't be.[80] Ask the person in charge of the library to get them. If the school library won't get them, club together with some friends to buy them for yourselves. Or ask for them in your local public library: public libraries are supposed to get any book you want to read, although this may take a little time.

---

77 This booklet is still around, though it costs more like £28 than 28p through second-hand booksellers. The National Secular Society still exists (www.secularism. org.uk) and they still campaign for better sex education.
78 Still available second-hand.
79 Still available second-hand.
80 In the 40 years since this book's publication there have, of course, been a multitude of sex education books published and you would be wise to check what is actually in your school library.

Venereal disease

One of the things most sex education books don't give proper information about is sexual disease (venereal disease or VD).[81] You can catch VD/STI if you have intercourse with someone who already has it, and you in turn can pass it on to someone else. VD/STI can be irritating but it's not usually serious and it can always be cured.[82] Like most other illnesses, however, the sooner it's treated the faster it's cured. So if you get a rash or sore on or around your sexual organs and you think you may have caught VD/STI or something similar, go to a friendly doctor at once, or to something like the local sexual health advisory service. The most common type of VD is gonorrhœa; syphilis, a much more serious type, is less common.[83]

---

81 Usually known these days as 'sexually transmitted infection' or STI; subsequent mentions of STD changed to VD/STI.

82 This is not necessarily true. HIV/AIDS (which was discovered after the publication of this book) is a lifelong and sometimes fatal condition. Other STIs can have lifelong effects too including infertility, problems in pregnancy, cancer and heart and respiratory conditions.

83 These days chlamydia and genital warts are the most common and genital herpes, gonorrhoea, syphilis and hepatitis are also found. HIV/AIDS has also had a major impact in the period since this book was written.

There's a strange "conspiracy of silence" about VD/STI in Britain. Advertisements about treatment for it are forbidden in open public places. But you can usually find notices about hospitals where you can go for treatment in public lavatories, i.e. where only one sex sees them at a time.

Abortion

If you use contraceptives it's unlikely that you'll get pregnant. Unwanted pregnancies usually occur because you haven't used contraceptives, either through ignorance or carelessness.

The first sign of pregnancy is usually that the periods stop. But menstruation can occur even if you are pregnant, and it can stop even if you're *not*. Girls often miss a period or even several periods just because they think they have become pregnant and are very frightened about it.

If you think you're pregnant, go to a doctor. But remember that even a doctor's first test can occasionally give the wrong result, so you may need a second test.[84] Alternatively you can find out quickly by using a pregnancy testing agency. This

84 Pregnancy testing is extremely reliable these days. You can buy a test for a few pounds in a chemist or supermarket and test for yourself. Free pregnancy tests are available via your GP, any contraception or sexual health clinic, young people's services or NHS Walk-In centres.

usually costs £2. Look for the advertisements in something like *The Observer* or the *New Statesman* (you can find these in your public library if necessary).

Remember, doctors are required to keep to their professional code, which means among other things that they must respect the confidence of their patients. As long as you are over 16 (the official "age of consent") you can go to your doctor to ask about abortion, in strict confidence.[85] Even if he disapproves violently and refuses to help you, he can't tell your parents without your consent. Doctors can be sued for breach of confidence.

A child has a right to grow up in good conditions. If you're very young or don't have much money or education and have a child, the child may have a very difficult life. In this sort of situation it's no wonder that some people panic if they find they're pregnant. But try not to panic. There are many ways of getting help.

If you do get pregnant, it's best if you can talk to your parents about it first. They may be shocked initially, but the chances are that they'll want to help when it really comes down to it. But if they won't help, or if you don't dare tell them or just don't want to, get in touch with the Student

---

85 See note 56 on page 107.

Advisory Centre[86] or Release[87] (addresses on page 127).

Legal and illegal abortion

If you decide it's better not to have the baby, you can have the pregnancy stopped. This is called abortion. Abortion is a minor operation: it can be uncomfortable, but it's not very dangerous if performed in time by properly qualified people. There are two kinds of abortion, legal and illegal. This is because the law in Britain doesn't allow a girl to decide herself whether to have an abortion or not. In some other countries the girl does decide herself: this is called having "free abortion". There will be "free abortion" in Britain too sometime in the future.[88]

At present, you can get an abortion on the National Health or in private clinics. In both cases the law says that two doctors must agree that the abortion is necessary. Some doctors are much more sympathetic than others. They're not obliged by law to agree to abortions. If the first doctor you

---

86 Again, this organisation doesn't exist but all colleges and schools will have someone who can help. Alternatively, the British Pregnancy Advisory Service, Marie Stopes or Brook can help.

87 This organisation no longer exists. There is another organisation called 'Release' – see the section on Drugs.

88 The 1967 Abortion Act still stands in the UK.

try won't agree, there's nothing to stop you trying others. Or contact the Student Advisory Service or Release.

In some areas so many doctors refuse to agree to abortions that it's very difficult to get one. In Birmingham, for instance, this has led to the creation of a special voluntary agency called the Birmingham Pregnancy Advisory Centre (address on page 127).

The Abortion Act of 1967 says that doctors can allow an abortion if having a baby would involve serious risk to the life of the mother or to her physical or mental health. In reaching their decision, the doctors can take into account a girl's present or probable future circumstances (i.e. the girl might be only 13, or have no means of supporting herself and a baby). This really means that doctors have a lot of discretion: one doctor might see no objection to you having a baby while you're only 16 and still at school, while another might consider this more than enough reason for having an abortion.

Some doctors may agree that you need an abortion but try to persuade you to have it in a private clinic. This may cost over £100. If you're legally entitled to an abortion, you should be able to get it on the National Health.

Legal abortion is safest. If it's carried out by a doctor under the right conditions it's no more risky than birth. But abortions performed by unqualified people can be extremely dangerous. There are many people who perform illegal abortions. Few of them have enough knowledge about it, and most of them work under unhygienic conditions. So don't use "any old address".

If you've had an illegal abortion and you notice the slightest thing wrong afterwards – if, for example, you start bleeding, feel weak or listless, or have pains – you must go to a doctor at once. You can safely tell him what's happened (but you needn't tell him who did the abortion). The doctor has a duty to help you or send you to hospital if necessary, just as if you'd had an ordinary accident.

Remember

If you want to get an abortion, you must start *as soon as you discover you're pregnant*. Even if everything goes smoothly, it will take some time to get through all the formalities.

Some doctors will try to put you off until it's too late to have an abortion at all. Putting you off is almost the same as refusing. Try another doctor immediately.

You should be prepared to meet hostility. In many places people take the opportunity of preaching morals at you or get at you in other ways.

Many girls get so desperate that they try to bring on the abortion themselves. There are many old wives' tales about how it can be done. Don't believe in them. Don't try it. You may kill yourself.

Methods of abortion

The "early abortion" is called "scraping" and can be carried out within twelve weeks of the last period. The tiny foetus is removed from the womb. This operation can only be performed in a hospital or clinic, and you normally have to stay on for a couple of days after the scraping. British hospitals are also starting to use a new and much quicker method, using an instrument called a vacuum curette.

The "late abortion" is carried out between the twelfth and the sixteenth week by injections into the womb.[89]

---

89 Abortions today are done using a pill up to 9 weeks of pregnancy (this is called an 'early medical' abortion). After 9 weeks and up to 20 weeks the pills can also be used but at a higher dose and it takes longer (this is a 'late' medical abortion). There are also surgical methods with vacuum aspiration/suction being used up to 15 weeks and surgical dilatation and evacuation (D&E) after that.

Addresses for advice and help on sexual matters[90]

The letters after each address show what the organisation can help you with, as follows:

a abortion
c contraceptives
h homosexuality
i impotence or other sexual difficulties
1 lesbianism
p pregnancy tests
v VD

Albany Trust *h, i, 1*
www.albanytrust.org 020 8767 1827

British Pregnancy Advisory Service *a, p*
www.bpas.org 03457 304030

Brook *a, c, p, v*
www.brook.org 0808 802 1234

Family Planning Association *c (over 16s only)*
www.fpa.org.uk

Stonewall *h*
www. stonewall.org

Lesbian and Gay Switchboard *1 h*
www.llgs.org.uk

---

90 This list has been updated. The following organisations listed in the original edition no longer exist: BIT Information Service, Gay Liberation Front, Release and Student Advisory Service.

London Pride *1 h*
www.prideinlondon.org or your local pride
movement

Kenric *1* www.kenric.org

Marie Stopes c
www.mariestopes.org.uk 0845 300 8090

The National Council for the Unmarried Mother and her Child[91] works to improve the status and condition of unmarried girls and women who have children. It refers girls to appropriate local agencies, but gives direct help if these agencies are not sympathetic. At the moment it is urging the government to improve conditions for mothers under 16. This is the organisation to contact if you get pregnant and decide you want to keep the baby.

All of the above organisations such as the FPA, BPAS, Brook and Marie Stopes can point you in the direction of further help if you decide to keep a baby.

Other organisations

NHS Choices Sexual Health
www.nhs.uk/Livewell/Sexualhealthtopics/Pages/
Sexual-health-hub.aspx

Sexwise helpline 0800 282930

Terrence Higgins Trust www.tht.org.uk

Childline www.childline.org.uk 0800 1111

---

91 It became 'Gingerbread', see www.gingerbread.org.uk.

Drugs

Drugs are poisons which can have a pleasant effect. People use drugs in spite of the fact that they can have bad effects, either because they simply don't know about these bad effects, or because they think the risks are less important than the pleasure that drugs can give.

Many, if not most people who use drugs start using them because their friends do. A lot of people go on using drugs for the same reason, rather than because they really need to or because they find the effects of the drugs really exciting. So using drugs, like many other common activities in life, is a social habit. Social habits are not harmful in themselves, but they can be indirectly harmful if the particular habit has bad effects.

Drugs can harm you in two ways. They can affect your body directly. And they can be habit-forming or addictive, which means that you can become mentally or physically dependent on them. The direct effects of drugs on the body are mostly on the blood, the central nervous system and the muscles. Most drugs have a very quick effect. They can also have long-term effects, damaging arteries, brain, heart, lungs, etc.[92]

---

92 Drugs can also be fatal. The long-term effects in the
    form of physical or mental disease can kill you over

Different types of drugs[93]

Stimulants
  Coffee
  Tea
  Tobacco
  Khat/Qat*
Inebriants
  Alcohol
  Marijuana/Cannabis*
  Hashish
Psychedelic drugs
  LSD
  Mescalin
  Magic mushrooms*
  Salvia*
Narcotics
  sedatives or
  barbiturates
  Sleeping pills
  Tranquillizers
  Phenobarbitone
  Nembutal

---

  time but a single adulterated (messed-with) or super-
  strong dose, or even just a new drug that doesn't suit
  you, could also lead to instant death. Overdosing is not
  uncommon amongst drug-users.
93 The drugs marked with an asterisk have been added in
  this edition.

Amytal
Soneryl
Benzodiazepine (benzos)*
Rohypnol (roofies)*
Valium*
Temazepam*
amphetamines:
stimulants or pep-pills
Benzedrine
Dexedrine
Methedrine
Preludin
Drinamyl
Ecstasy ('E' or MDMA)*
Mephedrone*
Speed (amphetamine sulphate)*
Methamphetamine (Crystal Meth/Ice)*
Alkyl nitrites (Poppers/Amyls)*
Ketamine*
strong narcotics or "hard drugs"
Opium
Heroin
Morphine
Cocaine and crack cocaine
Pethidine
Technical poisons or "sniffers"
Spirit glues

Cow gum[94]
Meths
Pure spirit
Cleaning fluids
Aerosols*
Nitrous oxide*

This is neither a complete list of drugs nor a universally agreed classification of the various types. Some experts might classify marijuana and hashish as psychedelic drugs or narcotics. Others think that some forms of alcohol should be classified as narcotics. The list above is intended only as a rough guide to the different types of drugs.[95]

Habit-forming, dependence and addiction

Most drugs create some form of dependence. This means that after using them for some time you can't do without them, either psychologically or physically or both.

You may become psychologically dependent on drugs if you take them to try to solve your problems. Even though drugs can't actually solve any problems, they may seem to make life more

---

94 Cow Gum used to be used by publishers for literally 'cutting and pasting'. Not available any more.

95 Further information can be found at, for example, Talk to Frank (www.talktofrank.com) or Drugscope (www. drugscope.org.uk)

bearable and you get into the habit of taking them. If you don't go on taking them you may get very depressed, and feel sluggish, apathetic or even desperate – partly because the unsolved problems are still there, and may even have become worse than they were originally.

Some drugs make you physically dependent too. As time goes on you find you have to take more and more of the drug to get the same effect. This is because your body "gets used to" the drug. And if you suddenly stop taking it after using it for a long time you may become very ill or collapse altogether. This is called having "withdrawal symptoms". People who can't do without a drug are called addicts.

Tea and coffee

Most people drink many cups of tea or coffee every day, which makes it seem strange to describe them as drugs. But they do contain a form of stimulant drug. The effects are usually very mild, but quite a lot of people find that they can't get to sleep if they have a cup of coffee before they go to bed. And some people are advised by their doctors not to drink either tea or coffee, because it has a bad effect on their health.

Tobacco

The most expensive form of tobacco, ounce for

ounce, is the cigarette. Cigars are cheaper, and the cheapest form of all is pipe tobacco.

Tobacco contains the poisonous drug nicotine. Four minutes after the first drag on a cigarette the concentration of nicotine in the brain is at its highest. The nicotine takes half an hour to get out of your system.

Nicotine affects the central nervous system and therefore, among other things, the heart and the digestion. Nicotine makes the veins and arteries contract. This happens very quickly. This contraction reduces the supply of blood to the various organs, for example the brain. This means that you get less oxygen and other necessary substances, so your body doesn't function as well as it ought to.

The smoke you inhale contains a lot of tar, a poison which enters your body as a gas. It's absorbed into the blood-stream from the lungs, which means that you absorb less oxygen into your blood-stream. All your organs need oxygen, but when you smoke they don't get enough. They get tar instead. This means, among other things, that the brain cells get damaged. Our bodies have a lot of brain cells, but once they're damaged they don't recover, and the body doesn't replace them.

Tobacco smoke, and particularly cigarette smoke,

contains other substances as well as tar and nicotine. To get an idea of what goes into your lungs when you smoke, get someone who smokes to try an experiment. Get him to take a drag on a cigarette without inhaling the smoke and then blow the smoke out through a clean white handkerchief held over his mouth. The result may surprise you.

The substances in tobacco smoke can cause bronchitis, heart disease and lung cancer. The Royal College of Physicians produced a report on smoking in January 1971. They calculated that if present smoking habits continue, 50,000 people in England and Wales will die of lung cancer *every year* in the 1980s.[96]

Smokers are up to four times more likely to get lung cancer than non-smokers. The more cigarettes a person smokes each day, and the earlier he starts smoking, the worse the risks are. Someone who starts smoking when he's 15 is *five times* more likely to die from lung cancer than someone who starts at 25. A person smoking more than 25 cigarettes a

96 Smoking habits did not continue; smoking has been in decline since its peak in 1974. Lung cancer incidence and mortality began to decline in the 1970s and in 2011 15,700 men and 12,500 women died of lung cancer in England. However, NICE calculate that 120,000 people die every year from smoking, as people die not just from lung cancer, but, for example, from heart disease or chronic lung disease also.

day is twice as likely to get lung cancer as someone who smokes less than 14 a day. Smokers are twice as likely to die before they're 65 as non-smokers.[97]

These facts should be enough to put anyone off smoking. But it has other effects too. If you're a heavy smoker you can get nicotine poisoning. The symptoms of this are paleness, headaches, nausea and vomiting. If you're a heavy smoker over a longer period you can get chronic nicotine poisoning. The symptoms of this are restlessness, lack of balance, difficulty in sleeping, headache and possibly dizziness. You lose your appetite, your digestion is disturbed, you can get palpitations (very fast heart-beats), catarrh and a continuous cough and have difficulty in swallowing.

The tar and other substances in tobacco smoke get deposited in your throat and lungs. This can lead to bronchitis: the lungs get irritated and you cough and bring up phlegm. If the bronchitis becomes chronic, it may kill you. Nicotine makes the particles of your blood more liable to stick to each other and to the sides of the blood vessels. This

---

97 The basic gist of what these statistics are saying is still true. See for example www.nhs.uk/Livewell/ Lungcancer/ or www.cancerresearchuk.org/cancer-info/ healthyliving/smokingandtobacco/smoking-and-cancer or www.nice.org.uk/nicemedia/.../smoking_and_ health_inequalities.pdf.

can lead to thrombosis (clotting) of the blood and other heart disease.

People usually start smoking, and continue, as a social habit. But it's easy to become psychologically dependent on it, and there is some evidence to show that it may lead to physical dependence too. Many people who've got into the habit of smoking find it very difficult to give up, even if they know it's very harmful.[98]

If you haven't started smoking, don't. Some of your friends or other people at school may smoke themselves and encourage you or dare you to try it. Saying no is sensible, not cowardly.

If you've already started smoking, try to give it up while you're young. The longer you smoke, the worse your chances are, and the more difficult it is to give up. If you can't give up altogether, at least try to cut down gradually. And while you're cutting down, try to reduce the risk in the cigarettes you do smoke. Prick a few holes in the cigarette where you hold it: this will let more oxygen into the smoke. Change to filter tips if you're using plain cigarettes. Don't leave the cigarette in your mouth between puffs. Leave longer stubs: the nicotine and tar get

---

98 Smoking is not only harmful to the person holding the cigarette. We now know that passive smoking is also dangerous and this led to a ban on smoking in all enclosed public places (including pubs and bars) in 2007.

concentrated in the end nearest your mouth.

If you have to smoke some form of tobacco, smoke a pipe, or cigars. Because you don't normally inhale pipe and cigar smoke, the risks of getting bronchitis, lung cancer, etc. are much lower than with cigarettes.

If you do smoke, remember that the sooner you stop, the easier it'll be and the quicker your body will be able to start "clearing itself". The 1971 report showed that even if a person smokes up to 19 cigarettes a day for many years, if he gives up, his chances of dying from lung cancer will reduce within 10 years to the same level as someone who's never smoked.

Alcohol

People drink alcohol in various forms. Each form has a different strength or alcohol content. In order of increasing strength, the main types of alcoholic drink are: beer and cider, ordinary wine, "fortified" or heavier wine (port, sherry, madeira, vermouth, etc.), spirits and liqueurs (whisky, gin, vodka, brandy, etc.).[99]

---

99 Today young people are also likely to drink 'alcopops'. These are sweet, usually fruity and fizzy, drinks sold in bottles and they have a similar alcohol content to beer and normal-strength lager. Because they taste pleasant it is easy to drink lots of them and get drunk very quickly.

Drinking alcohol is very much a social habit. When people want to celebrate or relax and have a chat, they often go out to a pub or have drinks at home.[100]

Small quantities of alcohol affect the senses. It weakens your muscle control (you may feel tight around the mouth, hence the expression "tight" for someone who's had a bit to drink). You react more slowly and your faculties of imagination, originality and criticism are reduced (although you may *feel* quite the opposite). It can also affect your balance and reduce your sexual powers (while often increasing your sexual appetite). It sends some people to sleep.

If you drink quickly and a lot – for example half a bottle of spirits in one go – alcohol poisoning can give you a heart attack, which may kill you. Some grown-ups can do it without dying, but this is because they've been drinking heavily for a long time and their bodies have got used to alcohol.

Alcohol is both physically and psychologically habit-forming. If you keep your consumption

---

100 Drinking at home has increased enormously in recent years as alcohol has become more widely available through supermarkets, which are open all hours. 'Binge drinking' is a commonly heard term referred to the practice of drinking lots of alcohol in a short time with the purpose of getting drunk. Pubs often run 'happy hours' offering cheap alcohol which facilitate this.

under control, the social habit is not dangerous in itself. But if consumption increases it can cause problems, for example in the case of a family where the husband or wife spends so much money on drink that they can't support the children.

Physical dependence is a strong risk when consumption is large – and it's easy to drink too much if you're not strong-willed. People who become physically dependent on alcohol are called alcoholics. Curing alcoholism is a very difficult and painful process. When an alcoholic is deprived of alcohol he may become delirious and experience strong hallucinations (see ghosts, or imaginary animals, or hear screams, etc.): he may go through deep anxiety and severe physical discomfort. Too much drink can also cause a very painful disease called cirrhosis of the liver. Spirits are more dangerous in this respect than beer, although really heavy beer-drinkers can suffer too.[101]

Alcoholism is a very common disease. It is estimated that there are at least 300,000 alcoholics in Britain.[102] Alcohol also kills and maims people

---

101 Super-strength beers and ciders can be particularly dangerous in this regard as they are cheap and easy to drink in large quantities whilst containing high levels of alcohol.

102 The charity Alcohol Concern puts that figure currently at 1.6 million.

who may not drink at all. Drunken drivers are responsible for thousands of deaths and serious injuries on the roads of Britain each year.[103]

What is "being drunk"?

If you only drink a little, you'll only get mildly drunk (or merry, tipsy, tight or stoned[104]). This usually feels rather pleasant. You feel happy and lose some of your most common inhibitions, i.e. shyness. This can be fun because you dare to say and do some of the things you really want to. Being slightly drunk can stimulate conversation and companionship.

If you go on drinking – and you often do if you're slightly drunk, because you can't think very clearly – you get really drunk. You lose your self-control, you find difficulty in talking, your vision becomes blurred – you may even see double. You begin talking very loudly and may get rather aggressive – and you may lose so many of your inhibitions that you say or do things that you'll regret later.

If you still go on drinking – and people often do,

---

103 Since 1979 (when recording began) the numbers of fatalities and serious injuries from drink-driving have fallen by more than three-quarters. In 2012 there were 280 deaths. However, there are some indications that numbers may be on the rise again.

104 The word 'stoned' is now generally reserved for the effects of cannabis.

because when you're really drunk there's very little control or consideration left – you can become heavily drunk. This means in fact that you've got alcohol poisoning. You wobble around, you lose all control over your speech and movements, and you will probably be violently sick. You won't know what you're doing and may lose your memory, to the extent that you won't be able to remember afterwards what happened while you were drunk.

What is a hangover?

Being slightly drunk won't usually produce any after-effects. But if you've drunk a lot, you'll probably wake up with a headache, and it may be quite a violent one. You may also feel sick and be sick.

There's very little you can do about a hangover except wait till the poisoning is over. You may try pouring cold water over your head, getting some fresh air, having a brisk walk – but, strangely, none of these things seem to help very much. Since so many people drink, you'll get all sorts of advice about how to deal with a hangover – but none of it is likely to work. Beware of taking pain-killing pills: these can be very dangerous when you've got alcohol in your body.

The best thing is to avoid getting a hangover in the first place. Having a few glasses of milk before you start drinking alcohol may help lessen the effects. One of the effects of alcohol is to dehydrate the body. This lack of liquid affects the brain, and that hurts. You can make a hangover a little less bad if you drink two or three glasses of water before you go to sleep: this will compensate for the loss of some of the liquid in your body. If you eat something salty at the same time, it helps your body to retain the liquid, which is an added advantage.

Another way is to control the amount you drink. The body takes more than an hour to get rid of one drink. If you have a lot of drinks in a short period, it may be many hours before your body is clear.[105]

Should alcohol and tobacco be legal?

In view of all the bad effects mentioned above, it may seem strange that alcohol and tobacco are legal. You're not allowed in pubs unless you're at least 18, and shops aren't meant to sell tobacco to people under 16 (unless a child is buying it for an adult).[106] But grown-ups are legally entitled to drink and smoke as much as they want.

---

105 The issue of 'binge drinking' is now highlighted as a common social problem. It refers to people drinking large quantities of alcohol in a short period and usually ending up very drunk.
106 As of 2007 you have to be 18 to purchase tobacco. Children are not allowed to purchase tobacco for adults.

Drinking in moderation isn't harmful, but it's very easy to drink more than enough. Smoking tobacco, and particularly cigarettes, has been shown to be very dangerous, even in small amounts. There is also the fact that a lot of non-smokers find smoking a very anti-social and objectionable habit.[107]

Part of the difficulty in getting the situation changed comes from the fact that alcohol and tobacco are very highly taxed in Britain. The tax on a £2.75 bottle of whisky is £2.20:[108] on a 31p packet of cigarettes the tax is 24p.[109] The government gets about £850 million a year from alcohol taxes, and almost £1.2 billion from tobacco taxes.[110] Together, alcohol and tobacco taxes make up almost 15 percent of total government income.[111] Few politicians relish the prospect of trying to raise that much money from other forms of taxation.

---

107 And, as was pointed out earlier, we now also know that passive smoking is dangerous to health.

108 Today whisky costs more like £20 a bottle and the duty is £7.90.

109 Cigarettes cost about £6–£8 for a pack of 20 and the duty is £3.80

110 Latest figures show that the government takes £10.2 billion in alcohol receipts and £9.68 billion in tobacco taxes.

111 Current HMRC figures show that tobacco and alcohol receipts make up 4 percent of total HMRC revenue.

(Incidentally, total consumer spending on alcohol and tobacco is more than spending on housing, including rent, rates, mortgages etc.)[112]

According to one estimate, the bad effects of smoking cost Britain £270 million a year.[113] (This includes £10 million as the cost of fires which are a result of smoking.) Tobacco is certainly the biggest killer in Britain today.[114] Something drastic obviously ought to be done to cut down smoking.

What happens at the moment is that the government pays for an anti-smoking campaign. But only £100,000 a year is spent on this,[115] while the tobacco industry spends £50 million a year

---

112 This is no longer true. ONS figures for 2013 show consumer spending on alcohol and tobacco at about 3 percent compared to 25 percent reflecting the massive increases in housing costs over the last 40 years (and the relative cheapening of alcohol).

113 Current estimates put this figure at more like £14 billion of which £507m is spent on dealing with fires.

114 Today's 'biggest killers' are heart disease, lung disease, strokes, cancer and liver disease. Clearly tobacco can be a contributory factor in most of these, but so are other factors such as obesity, sedentary lifestyles, stress and poor nutrition. ASH reckon that smoking is still 'the primary cause of preventable illness and death'.

115 The campaign 'smokefree' in 2013 cost £4.75m, with £2.7m of that spent on advertising. ASH estimate that £380m a year is saved by the NHS as a result of public health strategies.

advertising its products.[116]

Cigarette advertising on TV was banned in 1965. More action will now probably be taken to reduce smoking[117]. Possible measures include banning all other forms of tobacco advertising, stepping up the anti-smoking campaign, and perhaps making cigarettes too expensive for most people by doubling or trebling the present tax on them.[118]

If nothing is done and smoking habits continue unchanged, 25,000 children who are now at school will eventually die of lung cancer. Make sure you're not one of them.

Marijuana and hashish

Marijuana and hashish both come from a plant called cannabis or hemp. Marijuana comes from the top of the plant and looks like a sort of finely-

---

116 Tobacco advertising has been banned in the UK since 2005. Tobacco displays are now prohibited in large shops and supermarkets (so that packages cannot be seen), and will be banned in small shops from April 2015. There are current investigations into the merits of plain packaging for tobacco products, as used in Australia.

117 See note 116 above.

118 All of these have been done but there are still 10 million smokers in the UK. Other initiatives include the smoking ban (prohibiting smoking in public places), reducing the amount of smoking on TV/films etc and the introduction of e-cigarettes.

cut green tobacco. Hashish is from the resin and comes in lumps of various colours. Other names for marijuana and hash are pot, weed, or grass. Pot has been used as a stimulant since 2700 BC, and its use is very common in the Far East, the Middle East, North Africa and parts of Latin America.

The lumps of hash are warmed and crumbled, and can be mixed with cakes or tea, or smoked, either pure or mixed with tobacco. Smoking it produces the quickest effect, and has the advantage that you can stop when you notice the effect, which usually starts after a few minutes. The effect increases for half an hour and finishes, if you don't take any more, after about an hour and a half. It often doesn't seem to have much effect the first couple of times.

If you eat it, it takes longer to become effective, but the effect will last a lot longer. Some of the effects may be very uncomfortable if you eat it, since you can't regulate the amount after it's started to work. So it's easy to take too much.

Various types

There are many types of cannabis. There are two types from the Lebanon – one reddish-brown, the other light brown. There's a grey-brown type from Turkey and a dark-brown type from Pakistan. Mexico produces a type which is almost black.

The different types produce different effects, as well as tasting different. Hash produces the same kind of effects as marijuana, but it's stronger and the effects last longer. Their effects are easy to distinguish from the effects of alcohol.

What is "being high"?

Being high (or stoned) is the mood one gets into after smoking pot. You notice your body becoming more relaxed. Your muscles seem to function more slowly. Your pupils dilate. You speak more slowly. Your senses seem more acute. You see your surroundings in a different way. You can't take in much at once, but what you do see and hear seems more significant. Colours seem brighter. Objects seem clearer. You think you understand other people better than usual – even without anything being said. But if you take too much, these comfortable, pleasant effects disappear.

The effects may vary according to the mood you're in beforehand. They also vary from person to person. It's rare for anyone to become violent – which often happens when people get drunk. But with big doses it is possible to lose your self-control completely and act violently. With smaller doses, the most common effect is either that you become more withdrawn and introspective, or that you become friendly and happy and even giggly. You often get a dry mouth too, and want a drink – though hardly ever alcohol. Sexual feelings may either increase or decrease. Unlike alcohol, pot doesn't give you a hangover.

Does pot make you ill?

Being high is of course an abnormal condition, but it can hardly be called being ill. Pot can make you ill, however, if you've been feeling off-colour or slightly unwell beforehand, if you've been drinking alcohol, if you're sad or emotionally upset, or if you take too much. Once you get high it can be difficult to know when to stop, which means you may make yourself ill by taking too much.

Some doctors think that pot can delay your physical development if you smoke it when you're very young.

Is pot habit-forming?

Pot is certainly socially habit-forming, rather like alcohol or tobacco. People often smoke it for the first time when it's handed round at a party, and then go on smoking it whenever they're in similar surroundings.

If you're dissatisfied with your life and use pot as an escape, this can strengthen the habit – and you're on the way to psychological dependence. If you use it for a long time and in big doses you may get depressed and become rather listless and nervous if you suddenly stop. But studies of the effects indicate that psychological dependence on pot isn't so strong as it can be on alcohol or tobacco.

As for physical dependence, a World Health Organisation study in 1964 reached the conclusion that pot does not produce physical dependence, although continued excessive use of it can have harmful effects.

Is pot dangerous?

There's no definite answer to this yet. Some experts say that pot is much less harmful than alcohol or tobacco. Others say it can cause damage to the brain or nervous system. What evidence there is suggests that it isn't dangerous unless it's taken in excessive doses. But a lot more research will be needed before anyone can be certain.[119]

Because the effects are uncertain and because, unlike alcohol and tobacco, pot is relatively new in Britain, it's illegal.[120] This creates special dangers. Because it's illegal, there's no control over exactly

---

119 There is still a degree of uncertainty, although there is now more evidence that for some people cannabis use is harmful.

120 And is still illegal. It is currently a Class B drug, having been downgraded to Class C for a brief period leading up to 2009. There are campaigns to legalise it e.g. the Clear Campaign (www.clear-uk.org)

what is sold to whom. And in order to get pot people may have to contact "pushers" or criminals who often sell hard drugs as well. These hard drugs or narcotics have very different effects to pot and are known to be extremely dangerous.

Since pot hasn't been proved to be more dangerous than alcohol or tobacco, it might be better to make it legal. This would greatly lessen the risk of "pushers" leading people onto hard drugs, and would make pot easier to control, easier to study properly and hence less dangerous.

One particularly bad effect of the present ban on pot is its effect on the behaviour of the police. They have the right to stop and search anyone if they have "reasonable grounds for suspicion" that they're carrying drugs. Some policemen use this as an excuse to harass any young people who have long hair or "look like hippies" and therefore don't conform to their ideas of a "respectable citizen". They recently found it necessary to seize 4,000 copies of an "underground" magazine as a prelude to charging its editor with illegal possession of drugs. This is scarcely the best way of improving community relations and bridging the gap between young people and adults.[121]

---

121 The powers of the police to 'stop and search' are still an ongoing issue.

If pot was legalised, it would eliminate most of the artificial glamour and mystery that are sometimes associated with it. Remember that, legal or illegal, pot is only another artificial means of getting a pleasant sensation. It can't actually solve any problems you may have, in fact it may just make them worse.

LSD (acid) and mescalin

The effects of mescalin and LSD (or acid) vary enormously from person to person. There are cases of people who have taken LSD regularly over long periods without any apparent bad effects. There are also cases of people who have become incurably mentally ill or have committed murder or suicide after trying it just once.

LSD is a colourless, tasteless liquid. Mescalin comes from the juice of a small cactus. Both drugs are usually taken orally. The LSD dose (or "trip") sold on the illegal market is usually far too big. For mescalin, the "right" dose varies from person to person. The effects of the right dose of LSD start after about half an hour and may last for up to eight or nine hours. They may be followed by up to sixteen hours without sleep. The effects of mescalin start after two or three hours and last about twelve hours. With larger doses the effects start earlier and last longer.

LSD brings about changes in the biochemistry

of the brain and can lead to serious mental upheavals. It has become known as a psychedelic or mind-expanding drug, and some people think it can enrich their lives and bring new spiritual experiences. Some doctors have used LSD in treatment of patients with psychological problems. When you read about wonderful experiences as a result of using LSD or mescalin, they may well be true – for the individuals concerned. When you hear about people who kill themselves or go mad after taking it, this is equally true for them.

Some studies indicate that these drugs may cause damage to chromosomes or change their structure. This means that people who use them may produce deformed or mentally handicapped children. Even very small amounts of LSD are dangerous, since a fraction of an ounce can produce 10,000 doses.

There are two other drugs, similar to LSD, which are also used to produce a psychedelic experience. They are called DMT[122] and STP.[123] The effect of STP is similar to that of some nerve gases used in chemical warfare. It can have more dangerous and lasting effects than LSD, and if someone who has taken STP is given the drug Largatil to quieten him in hospital he may die.

---

122 Also known as ayahuasca.
123 Also known as DOM and similar to mescalin and amphetamines.

Remember

If you get high you think you're concentrating very hard and being very attentive. This may be true. But it's not you yourself who decides what you're going to be attentive to. Quite trivial things in your surroundings often impose themselves on you and demand your concentration.

Being high can be fun. But don't count on working or learning anything while the sensation lasts.

Narcotics

Many narcotics are used medically. But in recent years greater and greater care has been taken with them, since it's been shown that drugs such as morphine which were once thought to be harmless are in fact physically habit-forming and dangerous.

Amphetamines or pep-pills

There are many types of pep-pill, such as Benzedrine, Dexedrine, Methedrine, Preludin and Drinamyl.[124] They all have legitimate medical uses, but are also used illegally, "for kicks". Most of them have nicknames, such as "blues" (these used to be "purple hearts"), "black bombers", etc. These drugs

---

124 Today people would probably also have heard of Ecstasy ('E' or MDMA), magic mushrooms, Mephedrone, Speed (amphetamine sulphate), Methamphetamine (Crystal Meth/Ice), Alkyl nitrites (Poppers/Amyls) and Ketamine.

154

are usually taken in tablet form, but they can also be injected into the blood or breathed in from a spray.

The effects of small doses are strong beating of the heart, contraction of the blood vessels, widening of the pupils and loss of appetite. The drug often also makes you feel exhilarated and full of energy, confident and optimistic. Some people take them before exams because they think they'll make them think and work better and faster. But in fact they affect your judgement and make you less able to criticise your own work. When the effects wear off you'll feel a big come-down – you may feel exhausted, shattered and miserable.[125]

The effects of larger doses are dryness in the mouth, nose and throat, headache, feeling and possibly being sick, wanting to pee a lot, trembling hands, and an inner feeling of anxiety and disquiet. You can't sleep and may be gripped by fear.

Pep-pills are considered to be very strongly psychologically habit-forming. It's easy to acquire the habit, as you keep needing bigger and bigger doses to get the desired effect. When the need for sleep is decreased, your body becomes utterly

125 Since this book was written is has become possible to buy (legally) stimulants which have similar, though less potent effects, such as caffeine pills and 'energy drinks' containing taurine and caffeine, such as 'Red Bull'.

exhausted without you noticing it. With serious misuse there's a great risk of mental illness and paranoia. Misuse over a long period also reduces sexual desire and potency (the ability to have an erection).

Pep-pills aren't quite so difficult to come off as, for example, morphine, but you do need special treatment. You can't do it on your own.

Morphine

This is a pain-killing drug which also helps relieve nervousness, restlessness, anxiety and extreme unhappiness. It comes in tablet form or as a liquid which can be injected.

The effects vary from person to person. Many people feel sick and even are sick, although their pain disappears. Others find that morphine makes them pleasantly high.

If used over a long period, morphine becomes part of the metabolism – it's physically habit-forming. So the effects of stopping suddenly are very unpleasant. In fact they're so uncomfortable that many people on morphine go on taking it not because they want to get high but because of their fear of the withdrawal symptoms. People start taking morphine either during medical treatment, as a painkiller, or to experiment at parties. It's easy to get hooked on morphine, and it must be described as a highly dangerous drug.

There are substitutes for morphine, such as pethidine. These substitutes are used much more commonly than morphine itself because their side-effects are less unpleasant. But they are just as dangerous.

Opium and heroin

Opium is a well-known drug that has been used for many centuries, both medically and for pleasure. There are still large numbers of opium dens in many parts of the world, particularly in the Far East: in these dens, addicts lie on beds in small cubicles and smoke opium in special pipes.

Opium comes from a particular type of poppy. Morphine is one of the main ingredients of opium (codeine is another). Heroin is derived from opium, and is produced by heating a mixture of morphine and acetic acid.

Opium and heroin have similar effects to morphine. Heroin acts as a depressant: it lowers the level of nervous and other activity in the body. It's usually injected, and after the injection or "fix" the user immediately gets high and feels a sense of relaxation and freedom from the troubles of the world. It reduces the appetite and sexual drive, and for a long time the user will nod and doze and appear to be aimless and drowsy, but peaceful.

However, heroin is extremely addictive. Just one or two doses can be enough to get someone hooked. Once hooked, heroin addicts deteriorate rapidly, physically and mentally, and this tends to lead to an early death. A heroin addict is a slave to his drug: his whole day centres round getting his fix and he becomes incapable of doing anything else. He gets very ill if he can't get his fix and terror of this illness can make him go to extreme lengths to get supplies. It is possible to kick the habit in some cases, but only under intensive treatment and with terrible pain and withdrawal symptoms.

Heroin is often combined with cocaine to get a greater kick. This combination is known as H and C or "Speedball". A young addict may begin by "skin-popping" (injecting into the skin) and soon progress to "mainlining" (injecting into the veins, which gives a greater effect). The right dose is vital, since an overdose can easily kill.

Infection from a dirty needle is another serious risk (see *Injection*, page 163). Some addicts have difficulty in finding a vein to inject themselves, and this makes them sweat and scream and suffer physical and mental agony. As the veins get used over and over again for injection, they become scarred and unusable. As the larger veins collapse, the addict has to turn to smaller veins in arms or hands or legs.

People known to be addicted to heroin and other hard drugs in Britain are officially registered as addicts. This means that they can get supplies of their drug legally from certain doctors and clinics.[126] This gives the doctors some chance of trying to help them kick the habit. But it can enable some addicts to build up surplus supplies of their drug which they then sell to other people, thus making more new addicts. The number of known addicts in Britain almost trebled between 1961 and 1966, and the figure has gone on rising rapidly. By the end of 1969 there were over 1,200 registered addicts to heroin alone.[127]

Sick people or criminals?

However, the situation in Britain is certainly better than in the United States. In Britain an addict is recognised by the law and by the medical profession as a sick person. He is not a criminal

---

126 Heroin users are generally put on a prescribed methadone programme which aims to gradually reduce the amount of drug they take. They are not given heroin itself. There's no equivalent chemical substitute for cocaine but effective treatment consists of gradual detox combined with counselling and therapy to help deal with the addiction.

127 Calculating the number of people addicted to drugs is notoriously difficult, but the National Treatment Agency estimates that in 2011/12 there were almost 300,000 people addicted to opiates and/or crack cocaine.

unless he breaks the law to get his drug. But in America the use of narcotics is totally illegal. This has not produced a decrease in the number of addicts – quite the opposite, in fact. It has led to the growth of huge national and international criminal organisations which live on the illegal traffic in drugs.

From the poppy fields of Afghanistan, Iran, Turkey and elsewhere, opium is smuggled into somewhere like France; secret factories turn it into heroin and it is then smuggled into America and distributed through a huge network of pushers. Someone makes a profit on each little stage of this process, and the big criminal organisations make the biggest profit of all.

A further problem in America (and another source of profits) arises because the heroin used in the criminal industry is in powder form, which means that it can be, and is, diluted and mixed with things like milk, sugar and other more dangerous substances. Most of the heroin used in Britain is obtained legally on prescription and therefore comes in pure tablet form.[128] Another difference is that in America the vast majority of addicts are from economically deprived groups.[129]

128 Street heroin in the UK is generally 'cut' with something else, which may or may not be harmful.
129 Although celebrity and well-off heroin addicts make

They live in decayed, poverty-stricken areas of the cities, and the criminal activity associated with pushing and using heroin makes these slums even worse places to live in.

Very few doctors in Britain are willing to devote themselves to helping drug addicts, as this takes an enormous amount of time, energy and patience.[130] Many of them are, not unnaturally, reluctant to cooperate in what they see as an act of suicide by prescribing drugs which they know are killers. This in itself makes the problem worse, since addicts who can't get legal supplies tend to resort to the illegal market. With the number of addicts still increasing, the situation obviously isn't very good. But we do have at least the makings of a system to cope with the problem and perhaps, in the long run, to reduce it.

Opium and heroin remain extremely dangerous drugs. Keep away from them, and don't accept anything you're offered that may contain them.

---

the news, it is also the case in the UK that the majority of people with heroin addictions are from the lower socio-economic classes.

130 Whilst resources are limited there are now excellent drug programmes available and many more doctors are willing to help.

Cocaine

Cocaine is a stimulant and an inebriant. Dependence on it, like other drugs, can come about through social contacts, i.e. a casual offer or pressure from a group of "friends".

Cocaine is by far the strongest habit-forming drug. If you take it and then suddenly can't get any more you become mentally ill. This mental illness can become chronic or permanent. It's extremely difficult to cure, and can only be done in a mental hospital. Without treatment, misuse of cocaine will lead to total apathy and to psychological and social collapse. The number of suicides among cocaine addicts is five to six times higher than among people who take pep-pills, morphine, opium or heroin.

Sleeping pills and tranquillisers

There are many types of barbiturates, such as phenobarbitone, Nembutal, Amytal and Soneryl.[131] Doctors prescribe them as tranquillisers, sedatives and sleeping pills, but they tend to be more careful about them now than they used to be. People have become dependent on them and have taken larger doses

---

131 Modern day users would also come across benzodiazepines, Valium, Temazepam and Rohypnol (roofies).

than the doctor prescribed. Barbiturates are the most commonly used – or rather misused – drugs in Britain.[132] An overdose is fatal.

Technical poisons or sniffers

Some young people try to drug themselves by breathing in the vapour from spirit glues, solvents or cleaning fluids. This is dangerous and can kill you. These poisons damage the lungs, liver and brain – and induce symptoms of mental illness.

Injection

Drug addicts often share one needle to inject themselves without sterilising it properly. It's not enough to just boil it in the normal way. Using an unsterile needle leads to a liver disease called infectious hepatitis.[133] Even using an unsterile needle just once can lead to permanent damage to the liver.[134]

---

132 Barbiturates are less commonly used these days – benzodiazepines are more common (and often abused). But the most commonly abused drug in Britain is alcohol.
133 Or HIV/AIDS.
134 Many towns and cities have needle exchange services where people can get clean needles and other forms of support.

Remember

If anybody offers you pills, injections or types of pot you don't know, refuse them.[135] You can never be absolutely certain you're not going to get hooked. Remember all these drugs are illegal, so the people who push them make big profits: they may use all kinds of tricks and pressures to get you hooked.

If you do accept, you must understand that by doing so you are losing part of your freedom. This is the freedom to decide for yourself whether to stop or take more. It may change your whole life.

Before you start you're free. Afterwards you're not free: the drug rules your life. This has nothing to do with morals. Drugs act on you like this, it's the way your body, and particularly your central nervous system, is arranged.

Drugs won't solve your problems. The only way to solve problems is to change the things that cause them, not to try to escape or drop out altogether.

---

135 Since this book was written there has also been a rise in the use of 'date rape' drugs (some form of sedative), which are given to an individual without their knowledge, usually by dropping it in their drink. You should be careful who you accept drinks from and always keep your drink with you.

Books on drugs

Drugs by Peter Laurie (Penguin 25p)[136] is a reasonably accurate book that will tell you a little more about drugs and their effects.

The Release Report on Drug Offenders and the Law (Sphere, or from Release)[137] is a detailed report on how police and the courts deal with drug offenders. Any good public library should have other books on drugs which may also be useful.

Release was originally set up to provide legal assistance for young people arrested on drugs charges (mainly having or smoking pot). They're very overworked and desperately short of money, but do all they can to provide a really sympathetic and understanding service. If you get arrested on a drugs charge, contact Release or Street Aid.[138] All four organisations can help with general advice about drugs.

---

136 Still available second-hand.
137 Still available second-hand.
138 Release is still in operation but Street Aid isn't.

Addresses for help with drug problems[139]

Release
www.release.org.uk 020 7324 2989

Talk to Frank
www.talktofrank.com 0300 123 6600

DrugScope
www.drugscope.org.uk and
www.drugscope-dworld.org.uk

AddAction
www.addaction.org.uk

Childline
www.childline.org.uk 0800 1111

Drinkaware
www.drinkaware.co.uk

QUIT
www.quit.org.uk

---

139 This list has been updated. The following organisations
listed in the original edition no longer exist: BIT
Information Service, Street Aid and Student Advisory
Service.

The System

Your place of work

Grown-ups built your school and paid for it. They decide how things should be in the school. But it's you who use the school and first and foremost it's your place of work. Teachers work there too, of course, but if you weren't there they wouldn't have a job and wouldn't get paid. Teachers don't have to work in schools. You do. School is the only place where everyone in Britain must spend ten years of their life.[140]

You're not paid for your work, and unlike grown-ups you can't change your "job". So if you want a better school the only thing you can do is to start changing the one you've already got.

Remember, the local authority staff, teachers and other grown-ups who arranged your school and run it have some power, but not complete power. They may have the best intentions in the world, but find their plans frustrated by shortage of money (see *Education*, page 18).

The point is, though, that you still don't have much influence on decisions, let alone the right to

---

140 In fact everyone in Britain must receive an education for 13 years of their life. Most people's parents choose to send them to school, but the only legal requirement is that children are educated. This can be at home.

participate in decision-making. Far too often the authorities like to hang on to all the power, and as long as you don't know the system as well as they do, this is easy for them.

But nobody can control you completely if you don't want them to. They can't control your thoughts and opinions. They may perhaps get you to say what they want to hear – but you can think what you like and you can act as you think is right.

If a few of you get together you'll be much stronger, and you'll be able to influence things which grown-ups would otherwise decide on their own. No doubt you've often been told by grown-ups that the school is made for you. Yet it's usually arranged as grown-ups like it. Only a few schools are places that children and young people really enjoy being in. You can start changing this if you get together.

If your school looks like a shop window or a museum, it's because grown-ups are afraid of using things. Things mustn't get dirty or broken, they'd rather they stayed new. Often you may get the feeling that things are more important than people, instead of vice-versa. If your teachers are like this talk to them about it and try to get them to understand that all you want is to be allowed to use the school which they say is yours.

Classrooms

Most classrooms look like waiting-rooms or storerooms.

- In most classrooms the desks or tables are arranged in rows.
- You're often expected to sit in the same place all the time.
- The teacher is the only person who's allowed to move freely during lessons.
- The teacher is the only one who sits so that he can see all the faces.
- Only the teacher has his own cupboard and drawer.
- Plants and animals are rare.
- Comfortable chairs are rare.
- Radios and record-players are usually banned.
- Everybody has to go out during breaks.

It's not good if your school operates on these lines. Don't take this sort of situation for granted. If some of the things mentioned above are changed it will be to your advantage, and in the long run it will lead to much happier working conditions in the classroom. If you share your classroom with other classes, talk to them about it too.

Classrooms should be workshops, with work-tables, notice boards, shelves and tools for everybody. It should be possible to move the furniture around as needed.

Corridors

In most schools corridors are places for chasing children out of or through. In most schools corridors are boring places.

In some schools there has been some attempt to decorate them with pot plants, sculptures or pictures. This is obviously a good thing, but not if it stops you using the corridors for other things that may be more important. For example corridors can be used as somewhere warm and dry to stay in during breaks; as places for food and drink stalls; for exhibitions; as places to relax in, with comfortable chairs and mats or mattresses with cushions in the corners.

Playgrounds

Most playgrounds look like car parks or prison exercise yards.

An unwelcoming playground could be made fit for play and relaxation for less than the cost of one teacher's annual salary. There should be certain basic things in every playground.

A place to sit in peace and quiet. Areas where younger pupils can play and dig. Areas for playing football, running around, etc. Climbing frames, ropes, bats, balls, etc.

Think of other things yourselves and see if you can't get them.

One specially important point. In most schools the lavatories are bad. They're often filthy, and a few pupils bully everyone who goes in them. Teachers usually have separate lavatories. If everybody used the same lavatories, the conditions would certainly improve. At least demand that your lavatories are kept decent. Dirty lavatories are a danger to your health. Don't be put off by being told there's no money to make them better. This is one thing you really must insist on.

Other break-time activities

As well as using the playground, you should be able to do other things during breaks.

For a start, you should be able to use existing facilities like the gym, the swimming pool, the art room, music rooms, etc. There could be pop music in the hall for dancing. A lot of these places must, by law, be supervised. But you should be able to find some teachers who are willing to help.

There should also be rooms where you can sit and read, play chess or cards, or simply sit in the warm and chat. You should be able to use your classrooms for this.

Marks

Marks are used in schools as a kind of bribe, to get you to do things you don't want to do. A system based on marks makes you work for the marks – not because you enjoy the work and find it interesting. In some schools marks become an end in themselves,[141] just as money sometimes does in the outside world. The people who get the most marks (or money) are regarded as the best people, regardless of how and why they got the marks (or money) and what they're really like as people.

Are marks a swindle?

Marks can be a swindle. Marks can fool people – regardless of whether it's other people or you yourself who are fooled.

You fool others if you try to convince them that the mark is the only important thing about a piece of work. The importance of work lies in what you produce, what you create, what you learn.

You fool others if you try to convince them that they can know everything about a pupil from his marks.

You fool yourself if you believe that your efforts or your ability can be judged on a scale of 10, 20 or 100.

---

141 This culture of (over-) assessment is of considerable current concern. If anything things have got a lot worse over the past 40 years.

These marks can only tell you what you've learnt.

You fool yourself if, instead of judging a person by yourself, you believe that you can judge him from his marks.

Ask your teacher to tell you where your strength lies and where your weaknesses are, what you've learnt properly and what you still have to learn. And work out for yourself the most important thing: what really interests you and what doesn't interest you. This is what will be important when you leave school.

Some teachers think that marks tell everything about a pupil. This is nonsense. Marks may tell you something, in a crude and clumsy way, about how much you've learnt in a particular subject. But marks tell you nothing about your ability. Ability can't be counted like sheep or measured like wall-paper.

Marks do tell you something about a teacher. They tell you what he thinks of your work and what he expects of you (see *What a teacher expects of you*, page 85).

Marks are a means of power

Marks are also used to reward pupils or make them work harder. Pupils who may not know much about a subject but try hard are encouraged by being given good marks. Some clever but lazy pupils are given lower marks to persuade them to work harder. This means that the marks aren't being given as an impartial assessment of each pupil's work: the standards used for marking vary from pupil to pupil.

If marks are only used as a guide for the pupil, and the teacher explains to each pupil why he's given him a particular mark, this is acceptable. (Although you might well ask what is the point of giving a mark at all in this case.) But marks *aren't* usually explained to the pupils. Instead they're used to compare different pupils, and may even end up on a notice board, without any explanation. In this case marks are meaningless.

It doesn't make any sense to compare marks between yourselves. Marks themselves mean nothing. It shouldn't be a big competition. Never mind how other people do. Try to get the best out of each subject for yourself.

Against marks

In most schools teachers are forced to give marks. The authorities demand marks so that they can see how the teaching is going. And the exam system demands marks.[142]

---

142 Since this book was written more and more compulsory testing has been brought in with the SATs system (Standard Assessment Tests) which begins in Year 2 (6–7 year olds).

Don't accept marks as the be all and end all. And remember that there are many teachers who are fed up with the whole business of marks too. They realise that marks in themselves don't mean a thing. Talk to your teachers and try to find out what they think of marks. If they have a sensible attitude, tell them you don't want just marks (if you have to have them at all) but constructive comments on each piece of work, or a proper written evaluation of your term's work.

And ask them to talk to your parents. Because it's often parents who are most firmly convinced that marks tell you everything.

Exams and tests

Schools often use exams and tests to frighten you into working.

In some schools teachers believe that exams and tests can show exactly what you know. By far the greatest number of exams don't show what you know. They often ask the wrong questions. They may show what you've learnt parrot-fashion or had knocked into you. They rarely show whether you can think for yourself and find things out for yourself.

You can't rely on exam results at all. You're not allowed to discuss the questions with your friends. You may be nervous or ill at the time. You don't get enough time to think about the questions and write your answers. So it's not the people who know most who do best in exams: it's the people who are properly organised, can keep cool and can write fast.

In schools which have a lot of school exams and tests, education suffers. You don't learn about the subjects themselves: you learn how to cope with tests and exams.

This can be changed

Most schools still have exams at the end of every year. This wastes a lot of time, both for pupils and teachers. Try to get a big discussion going between teachers and pupils about these exams, and see if you can't get them abolished. It's up to each school to decide.[143]

If everybody seems to agree that it would be better to do without these exams but nothing actually gets done about it, try more direct methods. If possible, get everybody to simply boycott the exams altogether. If this is too difficult, everybody can turn up for the exams but simply hand in their papers blank. This will be a very effective way of getting the whole question properly discussed.

The school may agree to abolish, say, half-term or

---

143 Except that schools cannot choose not to participate in the SATs tests.

end-of-term exams, but insist on keeping end-of-year exams. If this can't be changed, the exams can at least be arranged differently. Pupils can be allowed to bring notes and reference books into the exams, or the exams can be held in a library where you're allowed to use the books during the exam. You can be told the questions in advance and allowed to prepare your answers. Quite a few schools have started to make changes like this in exams.

Public exams

Public exams are used at various levels of the education system to sort out the "sheep" from the "goats". They're used to decide who'll go on into the sixth form and who'll leave school or do a technical course or a secretarial course. They're used to decide who'll go on to college or university and who won't. There aren't enough higher education facilities for everybody, so exams are used as a form of rationing.

There are three main public exams in British schools. These are CSE (Certificate of Secondary Education), GCE O-level (General Certificate of Education, Ordinary level) and A-level (Advanced level).[144]

---

144 This system was changed in 1988 when GSCEs replaced O-levels and CSEs. A-Levels still exist but since 2001 they have been split into AS levels and A2 levels.

Normally in your 5th year[145] of secondary school you do either CSE or O-levels[146] in a number of subjects. If you don't do well in these, you may be encouraged to try them again – but this means staying down in the 5th form for another term or year. The chances are that this will be the end of your school education. 94 percent of boys and 88 percent of girls who get fewer than 5 O-levels leave school and go out to work. Even among those who get 5 O-levels or more, 73 percent of boys and 60 percent of girls still leave and start work.[147]

If you're among the minority[148] who do well in CSE or O-level and stay on, you'll go into the 6th form. Here you take A-levels in two or three subjects after two or three years.[149] (There is also a slightly higher level called S-level or Scholarship level.)[150]

A-levels are the rationing "sieve" for universities and other colleges of higher education. There aren't nearly enough university places for everybody

---

145 Now known as Year 11.
146 Now GSCEs.
147 The modern equivalent of '5 O-levels' is 5 GSCEs at grades A*–C. Today young people compulsorily stay at school until 17 and about 18 percent leave before taking A-levels/vocational qualifications.
148 No longer a minority.
149 Or a vocational course. Some schools also offer the International (or European) Baccalaureate.
150 These disappeared in 2001.

who wants one or could benefit from one.[151] So it's not even enough to get two or three A-level passes. They have to be good passes. If you don't get enough good passes, you may either have to do a subject you don't really want to do, or do your degree course at a college of technology, or forget the idea of getting a university degree altogether.

In Scotland the equivalents of O-level and A-level GCE are the Ordinary and Higher Certificates of Education. The Ordinary Certificate is the same level as GCE O-level. The Higher Certificate is a lower level than A-level, but it's done in more subjects.

11-plus

The 11-plus is another type of public exam which used to be used everywhere but is now being replaced by other forms of assessment in most areas. It's used at the end of primary school to select the small minority of pupils who will go on to grammar schools[152] (see *The British school*

---

151 University accessibility has been the subject of much development in recent years. Places were expanded and the old colleges of technology/polytechnics converted to university status in the 1990s. However, the removal of the grant system and the introduction of tuition fees and student loans in more recent years has made university attendance more financially daunting for many students.

152 Only some areas in Britain still have grammar schools and the 11-plus, such as Kent and Lincolnshire.

system, page 182).

Like other public exams, the 11-plus is a system of rationing – and a particularly bad one. Like other exams, the 11-plus can't measure real ability, let alone future capability. A lot of children don't start developing their knowledge and abilities properly until after they leave primary school. But the 11-plus selects on the basis of existing knowledge. So it often selects the wrong pupils, and condemns some of the most able ones to an inferior education in a secondary modern school. Like streaming within a school (see *Streaming*, page 88), selection at 11-plus tends to work in favour of middle-class children and against children from poorer or working-class backgrounds.

Can public exams be changed?

Public exams aren't an effective method of rationing, let along a fair one. Like any other form of exam or test, they tend to test knowledge rather than ability.

You're not allowed to take any books or notes into public exams. To get all your answers done in the time you're given, you have to write like a maniac. There's great pressure from your teachers and parents to do well. And you know yourself that you won't be able to "move on" if you don't pass.

All this builds public exams up into a really big

thing. The whole process is very nerve-racking. As a result, a lot of people get flustered and can't think straight or go blank or even go completely to pieces either during or before the exams. It's difficult to think of a worse way of giving everybody a fair chance to show what they're capable of. Some teachers and educationalists are strongly against public exams. Having to prepare their pupils for exams means that teachers can't teach what they really want to teach and what their pupils want to learn. Everything in the exam syllabus has to be covered, so there's no time during lessons to get diverted onto an interesting side-track and have a long discussion about something that's not needed for the exams. Public exams make teaching inflexible, and they only measure academic knowledge. They can't measure a person's real abilities and the contribution he may be able to make to society.

But most teachers still believe that exams are necessary. They say society can't do without some form of exam or other. Tell them that in Swedish schools all public exams have been abolished.[153] Ministry inspectors ensure that all schools keep up the same standards of teaching. Pupils do still get marks or grades, but these are based on all their work at school, not just on the results of a few

153 Finland also has no exams.

181

hectic hours of exams.

You may have some success in changing internal exams at your school, or even getting them abolished altogether. But it's much more difficult to get rid of public exams. This would involve a basic change in national education policy – and a basic change in the attitudes of most teachers and parents. A change this big will probably take many more years – but it will eventually come about.[154]

The British school system

Most countries have one basic state education system, with only a few private schools outside the state system. Britain has many different types of school.

There are independent schools, including kindergarten and nursery schools, junior schools, preparatory schools and so-called public schools. Some of these independent schools are run by religious organisations, others are run by private foundations.

Within the state system, established and run by Local Education Authorities, there are nursery schools,[155] primary schools (sometimes

---

154 It hasn't yet and in fact some people say British children are now some of the most tested in the world.

155 LEAs tend not to run 'nursery' schools as such, these are usually private. They do operate Early Years

divided into infant and junior), middle schools, grammar schools, secondary modern schools, comprehensive schools[156] and 6th form colleges[157].

Somewhere between these two main types, but basically considered part of the state system, there are various types of schools established and run by private organisations but financed, and ultimately controlled, by the LEAs or the Department of Education and Science. These include high schools, county schools and direct-grant schools.[158]

Finally there are various types of schools for backward or handicapped[159] children (special schools) and so-called approved schools[160] for

---

Foundation Stage education which covers pre-school and Reception classes.

156 Secondary modern schools (which were for children not considered 'clever' enough for grammar schools have disappeared. Secondary schools are now typically 'community schools', 'voluntary-aided schools', 'academies', 'free schools' or 'city technology colleges'.

157 Many schools have their own 6th forms or there are separate 6th form colleges.

158 See note 156.

159 Again, these terms are now out of use. There are still special schools but many children with disabilities are educated in mainstream schools with special support where needed.

160 Approved schools ceased to exist in the early 1970s, to be replaced with 'Community Homes' (now known as 'Secure Children's Homes').

children who get into trouble in the courts. (Courts also send young people to borstals,[161] but these are more like junior prisons than schools as such.)

Independent schools

At the moment about 10 percent of British children are educated in independent schools.[162] Parents usually have to pay fees to send their children to these schools. But Local Education Authorities sometimes subsidise the fees for individual children, or pay for and fill a certain number of places with children from the area.

Many preparatory (or prep) schools and public schools are boarding schools. The pupils live at the school during term-time – although there are often some day-boys or day-girls as well. Relatively few independent schools are co-educational.[163] Most of them take either only boys or only girls.

Some public schools are many centuries old. Many of them were originally set up to provide education for children whose parents couldn't afford to pay – hence the name public schools. They gradually became more exclusive and started charging

---

161 Borstals were abolished in 1982 and replaced with Young Offender Institutions.
162 Currently 6.5 percent of UK schoolchildren are educated privately and 18 percent of 16+.
163 80 percent are now co-educational.

fees. Some of them now charge more than £800 a year for each pupil.[164] In the early part of this century, public schools saw themselves as places for educating "leaders of men", the people who were meant to rule Britain and its colonies overseas. Some public schools still haven't got beyond this idea even today. Many of them still place most emphasis on "a healthy spirit of competition" and "qualities of leadership". Some parents are so eager to give their children this sort of education that they put them down for a place even before they are born, although the entry age is 12 or 13.

Some parents choose independent schools for their children for purely snobbish reasons: they don't want them to grow up like "common, ordinary children". Others are willing to pay the very high fees because they believe that their children will get better teaching than in a state school. Others believe that having a public school education will enable their children to get better jobs. Although things have changed a lot, there are still many places where "the old school tie" does seem to open doors that are closed to "ordinary" people.[165]

Some public schools can give their pupils more

---

164 The average yearly fee is now £14,295.

165 This still hasn't changed. Personal connections – who you know – and the 'old school tie' can still get you a long way, especially in certain sectors such as the City.

individual attention than other schools, simply because they have more money and can afford to employ more teachers. The average public school offers no better teaching than the average state school, and there are some public schools where the standards of teaching are way below the standards in state schools.

There is a lot of controversy about public schools. One argument public schools use is that they can provide facilities for children whose parents work abroad. But most LEAs have excellent boarding schools for children in this position.[166] Defenders of public schools say that parents should be able to choose freely where their children are educated. What this means in practice is that rich parents have freedom of choice, but poor parents have no choice at all.[167] Freedom of choice is not a bad principle in itself, but it's completely unjust if it simply means that rich people can buy a privileged education for their children.

NB. In Scotland (and America) a public school actually is a public school (i.e. a free, state school).

---

166 There are only 36 state schools which offer boarding (and the boarding is not free, only the education).
167 In recent times this argument has been extended to state schools as well, with accusations of rich parents 'pushing out' poorer parents in competition for places at the best state schools.

State schools

Compulsory education for all children begins at the age of 5, and is provided free of charge in state schools up to the age of 18. At present people can leave school once they are 15, but in 1972/1973 the minimum age will go up to 16.[168]

Most Local Education Authorities provide nursery schools for children between 2 and 5, but parents usually have to pay fees for these nurseries,[169] and there aren't nearly enough places for all children. (See *Streaming*, page 88, for the effects this has.)

But LEAs have to provide primary and secondary schools. Most primary schools are for children from 5 to 11. Some areas have infant schools for 5 to 7s, then junior schools for 7 to 11s.

Some LEAs still use the 11-plus exam at the end of primary school to decide how pupils will be divided in secondary schools. The academically brighter pupils go on to grammar schools. The rest – the majority – go to secondary modern schools[170] where the emphasis is more on practical things (technology rather than science, domestic

---

168 School leaving age was 16 for 40 years, but as of 2013 it went up to 17 and will go up again to 18 in 2015.

169 Most pre-school provision is privately provided but the government pays for 15 hours a week of preschool education for all 3 and 4-year-olds and some 2-year-olds.

170 Community schools.

science for girls, etc). In effect, the LEAs are virtually condemning the pupils who go into secondary moderns to the less skilled jobs which our society needs doing. The standards of teaching in secondary moderns are often lower than in grammar schools – and the teachers just don't expect their pupils to be bright anyway, so the pupils don't learn so much (see *What a teacher expects of you*, page 85).

But a lot of people disagree with the whole 11-plus system and object to its inefficiency and the social injustice it produces. In July 1965 the Department of Education and Science issued a circular to LEAs recommending that they should end selection at 11-plus and "go comprehensive".[171]

The idea of comprehensive schools is to really give every pupil equal opportunities in education. Comprehensives are generally bigger than other schools, so, in theory at least, they can offer a much wider choice of subjects. More of them are co-educational than grammar and secondary modern schools, so there is a more natural mixture of boys and girls. Comprehensives cater for pupils of all abilities from 11 to 18 and are intended to be much more flexible than the old grammar/secondary modern system. Pupils can in theory, work with

---

171 Which is exactly what most LEAs did.

different groups according to their ability in each subject. The wider range of social backgrounds and the more open atmosphere is meant to lessen the differences between "academic" and "non-academic" types – i.e. the class differences. But see *Streaming*, page 88.

Some comprehensive schools cover the whole 11–18 age range. Some are split into junior comprehensive (11–13/14) and senior comprehensive (13/14–18). Some cover the 11–16 range and are linked to separate 6th-form colleges (16-18). There is also a new type of school called middle schools. In this system, children go to one school from 8 or 9 to 12 or 13, then at 12/13 they move on to a senior comprehensive school.

Some LEAs are still refusing to change over to comprehensive schools. Others are changing over but keeping grammar schools as well, which defeats the whole purpose of comprehensives. Others have agreed to change in theory but are being deliberately slow in putting their plans into practice. About 50 percent of Scottish secondary pupils are now in comprehensives, but in England and Wales nearly 60 percent are still divided into grammar and secondary modern schools and only about 25 percent are in comprehensives.

School uniforms

Unlike schools in most other European countries, most British schools still make their pupils wear uniforms.

Most schools make parents sign a form of consent before they will accept their child at the school. The school's regulations on uniform are usually part of the form of consent. Even if the parents don't really want their child to wear uniform, they have to sign – or find another school. It's a form of blackmail.

Headmasters and other teachers who support the wearing of school uniforms claim that they help to disguise differences in parental income and encourage a sense of belonging to the school.

But in almost any school it will be obvious whose parents haven't been able to afford a spare uniform or regular dry-cleaning bills.[172] For parents with very little money, buying a uniform (often from a rather expensive shop which is the only one that has the uniforms) can mean not buying some other clothes. They can get a grant from the LEA – if they can "prove" that they're poor – but this has to be spent on the school uniform, not on other clothes which might be

---

172 Although today very few school uniform items cannot be machine-washed.

both cheaper and more hard-wearing.[173]

As for making pupils feel they "belong" to the school, there are surely more subtle and less superficial ways of doing this than making everyone wear a uniform.

Discrimination against girls

Throughout this book we've generally referred to both pupils and teachers as if they were all male. This is only to avoid repeating "he or she" each time. There are of course as many girls as boys at school, and there are almost 50 percent more female teachers than male teachers.[174]

Unfortunately, many schools seem to think that girls shouldn't be treated the same as boys. It's probably true for a start that girls-only schools don't attract such good teachers as boys-only schools.[175] And in most co-educational schools it seems to be assumed that the vast majority of girls will become either typists or housewives, or both.[176]

---

173 Many local authorities no longer provide 'uniform grants'. Schools are not supposed to force you to buy items from an expensive supplier, and many basic items are now available cheaply from e.g. supermarkets.
174 Currently 88 percent of primary teachers and 62 percent of secondary teachers are female.
175 In any case there are few single-sex state schools left.
176 Assumptions about what girls can and will become

While boys can do things like woodwork and engineering, girls are fobbed off with typing and domestic science.[177]

In this respect, schools reflect our society. It is remarkably difficult for a girl to find an interesting job once she leaves school, apart from a few things like nursing which are terribly underpaid anyway. If she looks around, she'll find there's very little choice apart from some kind of office work, production-line work in a light engineering factory, being a shop assistant – or starting a family.[178] Boys have much more choice.

If you want to do a subject that girls don't normally do in your school, just ask the teacher concerned or your head of house. You may be allowed to do it, without any difficulty. But if the answer is no at first, insist on your right to be treated like anyone

---

have seen enormous change in the 40 years since 1970. Girls frequently achieve better academic results than boys and many will go on to university and top jobs in all fields.

177 Today all subjects are studied by all genders, at least in KS3 before options are taken.

178 There are very few fields now which are closed off to women. However, there are still concerns about a pay gap between men and women doing the same job, about the 'glass ceiling' (women not reaching the very tops of their professions) and about the extreme demands of combining a career with motherhood.

else. Find out if there are other girls who want to do the same as you, and all ask together. Refuse to be discriminated against because of your sex. This applies after you leave school too.

Early specialisation

A lot of teachers and other people are concerned about what is called early specialisation. In most schools, pupils are obliged to pick particular subjects and drop others at various stages.[179] Some schools only allow pupils to do a certain number of O-levels, and they may have to decide whether to do a technical subject or a language. After O-levels, pupils who stay on at school have to choose two or three main subjects to do at A-Level (more in Scotland).[180]

Very few children can really know at the age of 13 or 14 which subjects are going to be most useful to them or most interesting. Even after O-levels it's often difficult to know which subjects you're best at: your interests may still be changing, or a subject

---

179 This still happens. Pupils in Year 9 (aged 14/15) will be asked to choose about 4 subjects from specified lists which they want to study to GCSE alongside the compulsory subjects.

180 Since the introduction of AS levels this has changed slightly with many students studying 5 or 6 subjects to AS and then continuing with the traditional 3 or 4 at A2 level.

that you've found a bit boring before may become much more interesting at a more advanced level.

It's not particularly easy to change subjects between leaving school and starting university, or once you've actually started university. The fact that a relatively large number of people do change suggests that our present system of specialisation doesn't work very well. And the fact that large numbers of university students still don't really know what they want to do even after they've finished their course suggests that it's idiotic to expect children of 13, 14 or even 15 to know what they want to do.

Staying on in the 6th form

At the moment, most schools only want pupils to stay on in the 6th form if they are going to go to university.[181] Part of the reason for this is of course that schools don't get enough money to offer more 6th form places. But part of the reason is that schools see themselves as part of the academic ladder, with the result that they concentrate only on academic things.

If schools really offered each individual a proper education (see *Education*, page 18), 6th forms would be open to everybody. They wouldn't be just

---

181 6th forms now typically offer vocational courses too to cater for students who will be going to work rather than university.

for pupils aiming at university, but for anybody who wanted to follow a particular subject or subjects up to a higher level.

It will be a very long time before this happens.[182] But it would be a good idea to get as much discussion going on as possible. If enough pupils and teachers in enough schools start questioning the present 6th form system, it should eventually get things moving nationally.

Meanwhile there are several things you should know about staying on after the school-leaving age. State schools are still free for pupils over 15, but for some pupils, staying on may cause hardship for their families. Parents who have a lot of children or get low wages or none at all (there were over half a million people unemployed in Britain at the beginning of 1971) may find it very difficult to go on supporting their children after 15 if they don't go out to work.

There is some provision for people in this situation. LEAs are allowed to make maintenance grants[183] to

---

182 Academic study at 6th form colleges is still only open to those wanting to take A-level (or IB) exams, usually with a view to entering university. However, there are many courses available at community colleges that are open to anyone.

183 England no longer offers Educational Maintenance Grants, but there are bursaries available for people on

pupils if staying on after 15 would otherwise cause hardship to their families. But there is no national regulation of these grants, so they vary widely from one LEA to another. Each LEA has its own standards for deciding who can get a grant, and its own actual scale of grants. A "good" grant is £3 per week – many are less.[184]

If this system of grants is ever to work properly and help everybody who needs help, there will have to be two important changes. There will have to be a standard national scale of grants. And the grants will have to be equivalent to a proper living wage for a person of that age.

Careers advice

A recent film called *Kes*[185] contains a very funny scene where the boy in the film is interviewed by the youth employment officer. The boy finds lessons boring, and he's hopeless at football: his only interest in life is a kestrel which he took from its nest as a baby and managed to train – a long and difficult process. When he gets into the interview, the employment officer obviously doesn't know anything about his school work, let alone his outside interests.

---

low incomes via the educational institution itself.
184 The Bursary Fund provides up to £1,200 a year.
185 No longer 'recent' but still available.

– Well lad, what would you like to do?

– Dunno.

– What about an office job then, good security, good steady job?

– No, too boring.

– Have you thought about an apprenticeship? The pay starts low, but you get a trade at the end of it.

– No, not if the pay's low.

– Well… have you thought about coal-mining?

– No, I'm not going down the pit, never.

Baffled, the employment officer gives him a standard leaflet about job opportunities and that's the end of the careers advice.

In the film it's really funny. In real life it's not at all funny, because it's all too true. All too many people get absolutely nothing out of school. They're not stupid or backward. It's just that the school has never managed, and perhaps never really tried, to stimulate them into discovering something they like doing, something they really find interesting.

All too many pupils find at the end of their school life that the careers master or the youth employment officer has nothing to offer them, or at least nothing they can raise any enthusiasm for.

All too many pupils find when they leave school that our society seems to have nothing to offer them except the dregs. They've been put in the lowest streams at school because nobody has had the time or patience to find out what they're good at. After school they find that without "qualifications" society can only offer them dirty, boring, dead-end jobs. They started school at the bottom of the social pile, and after ten years of so-called education they're in the same place.

Few schools provide a proper careers advice service. Some schools have some information, in the form of leaflets and booklets on this career and that one. But few of these leaflets seem to be written in good plain English, let alone tell you what you really need to know about the jobs. Besides, you need advice on which general areas may suit you best and be worth investigating further.

Some schools have a teacher who is responsible for careers advice, either full-time or part-time. But often these "careers advisers" don't have either the time or the patience for the big long discussions most pupils need to find out what would suit their interests and abilities best.

The local council runs a youth employment service,[186] with officers whose job is to help school

---

186 Local authority provision varies but most can offer something through the youth service/Connexions.

leavers find a job. They sometimes don't have enough time for proper discussion either, so often all they can offer is a production-line job in the local factory, a clerical job in a bank or the council offices, a future as a brush salesman – or a career "going places with the new army". In some areas there just aren't enough jobs for all the school-leavers.[187]

A special note about careers in the Army. The Army has a special boy apprenticeship scheme for boys leaving school at 15.[188] The advertisements in cinemas and elsewhere make army life seem rather glamorous and exciting. A lot of boys sign on full of enthusiasm, only to find that the life isn't so exciting from the inside. Once you've signed on for the minimum period, it's really difficult to get out again if you change your mind. And the years before you're 18 don't count towards your minimum period.

You may decide that you really do want to be a soldier. Think hard before you commit yourself,

There is also a national website: nationalcareersservice. direct.gov.uk.

187 Currently about 14 percent of young people aged 16-24 are 'NEETs' (Not in Education, Employment or Training'. Not all of these are unemployed, however, some are unable to work.

188 Girls can now join the Army and both boys and girls need to be 16.

though, and remember, whatever the adverts say, when it comes down to it, armies are concerned with killing. You may have to kill other people or get killed yourself, and you don't get any say in who you're meant to kill.

What can you do yourself?

Your last year of school should really be an initiation into the adult world of work. There are very few schools, if any, in which it works like this. This may be a result of lack of imagination rather than lack of willing on the part of the school. Try making a few suggestions.

See if the school will invite a trade unionist from a local factory to come and tell you about his factory and any other jobs he's done. If the school won't invite him officially, either invite him yourselves or meet him somewhere else for a discussion with a group of friends.

If the school doesn't arrange visits already, ask if you can be taken round some industries and offices in the area, or something like a big post office sorting office, a warehouse or a bank. Most "guided tours" like this try to show you only the best aspects of the place. But if you use your own eyes and talk to people working there you should be able to get some idea of what it would be like to work there yourself.

Ask your parents to tell you in detail about their jobs. Ask your friends' parents too, and other people in different jobs.

Remember that there are various forms of further education open to you outside school. If you want to get some more O-levels, or some A-levels, but don't want to stay on at school after 15,[189] you can go to a technical college and do them. If there isn't a tech near you, the Local Education Authority probably runs some suitable evening classes in most subjects. In some areas these classes are run in school or college buildings; others are run in the growing number of "village colleges".[190] Get details from the LEA – you'll find their address among the council offices in the telephone directory. (Or alternatively ask in the reference section of your local public library for the Education Committees Year Book; this gives not only the addresses of all LEAs, but the names of the various officers, sub-committees, etc. This useful book also lists every single technical college, area by area, other colleges and even secondary schools.)[191]

The National Extension College[192] is another

---

189 See note 167 on page 186.
190 Community colleges.
191 This information is now probably best accessed via the local council website or the library.
192 See www.nec.ac.uk.

organisation which can help you get O-levels[193] and A-levels. Their system works mainly through correspondence courses.

If you want to follow a subject beyond A-level, the new Open University may be useful to you. This provides university degree courses especially for people who haven't got the formal qualifications to get into an ordinary university. The teaching is done by correspondence, personal tuition and lectures on TV and radio.[194] If you want to actually do a degree you have to apply for registration, but you can watch and listen to a few of the TV and radio programmes first to see if it might be what you want.

You will also see a lot of advertisements in newspapers and magazines for various kinds of correspondence courses, and computer training courses "leading to highly paid, secure jobs". All these courses are run by private organisations for profit, and you often have to pay quite high fees. Relatively few of them offer anything more than you can get virtually free from LEA daytime or evening classes. Be particularly careful about the computer courses. The fees for these courses are very high, and even if the particular course does

---

193 GSCEs.
194 These days the Open University makes extensive use of the internet and other modern technologies too.

teach you computer programming reasonably well it's unlikely to help you get a job, since most companies using computers prefer to train their own programmers on their own machines.

The educational pyramid: who makes the decisions?

In school you notice teachers making decisions that affect you every day. But who controls teachers?

Bigger schools are divided into departments for teaching. Thus for example a maths teacher in such a school is responsible to the head of the maths department, as far as his lessons are concerned. The heads of department are senior teachers usually chosen by the headmaster. Heads of department may themselves choose deputy heads to help them.

Things that aren't directly concerned with lessons, such as general discipline, pupils' personal problems and maybe sports and the use of certain buildings, are often controlled by housemasters or heads of house.[195] Again these are usually senior teachers chosen by the headmaster and responsible to him.

The headmaster is chosen not by the teachers but

---

195 Although many state schools still have 'houses' these are less used for pastoral care. It is usually the 'Head of Year' or 'Head of Key Stage' who is in charge.

by the authorities (see below). He usually selects his own deputy, to make decisions if he is ill or away. Teachers have no more say than you in choosing the person who runs your school. But in most places they try to cooperate with him, even if they dislike his methods. Their only alternative would be to get transferred to another school.

The teachers have meetings at which they're meant to discuss things and agree on what to do. But very often these aren't proper discussions (see *What happens at staff meetings?* page 46).

In some schools cooperation among teachers is good, in others it's not so good. This may be because the teachers don't like the headmaster, or because various groups or cliques of teachers disagree among themselves.

Although the headmaster is the most powerful person in a school, he isn't entirely free to make his own decisions about everything. Major decisions have to be referred to the school governors.

In the state system, school governors are chosen by political parties.[196] The governors of independent

---

196 School governing bodies are made up of different types of governors. Some are appointed by the local authority, others are 'parent' governors, others are members of the local community who have been nominated and some are staff governors.

schools usually choose themselves. Many of both sorts, if not most of them, know nothing at all about education apart from what they can vaguely remember of their own schooldays. There is no provision for either teachers, parents or pupils to be represented on the board of governors. A few parents do become governors, but as a result of their position in the community, not because they are parents.[197]

Some schools have a parent-teacher association. These associations can't make any decisions about school policy. But they could be very useful by giving teachers a chance to find out much more about their pupils' backgrounds and problems, and getting parents much more actively involved in the actual running of the school. But schools seem to prefer to keep parents out of the running of the school. So parent-teacher meetings are rarely a lively two-way exchange of ideas and discussions. Instead one tends to find parents "discreetly" asking the teachers "how well Robert's doing" and then making polite conversation about the weather or last year's holidays. But a few more questioning parents, or an official delegation with a complaint from the pupils, could make even the dullest of parent-teacher meetings into a more lively and useful gathering.

---

197 This is no longer the case, see note 195 on page 203.

Higher authorities

The school governors decide or confirm the appointment of some teachers: other teachers are appointed by the LEA. The governors discuss plans for new buildings, make decisions about big items of equipment that have to be bought, etc. They are also entitled to question the headmaster's decisions and behaviour. But in practice few boards of governors go against their headmaster, mainly because the headmaster is the one person there who knows all about the school.

The governors decide how the money allocated to the school will be used. They don't decide how much money the school actually gets. (But they may be able to apply pressure and get an extra allowance for a particular thing like a building or a piece of equipment.)

The really big financial decisions are taken by the LEA. The LEA in turn is controlled by the local council, which decides how much money the LEA will get. The local council gets its money partly from local rates, partly from the central government. The Department of Education and Science (DES)[198] lays down the national guidelines for educational policy. LEAs put the national policy into practice as they see fit – which means that

---

198 Now known as the DfE, Department for Education.

there are some wide variations between different areas.

The national policies laid down by the DfE tend to be long-term policies. They are never put into effect very quickly. For example their circular of July 1965 telling LEAs to stop using the 11-plus exam still hasn't been carried out by some LEAs. The DfE decides important things like the number of teachers who are to be trained each year, school starting and leaving age, etc. As the DfE is a government department like any other, the amount of money it gets each year is decided by the government of the day.

The whole system is extremely complicated, and it means that things have to be discussed by a lot of different people at different levels before they can be carried out. If you have a serious complaint about a teacher or your headmaster or something else at your school, you may have to take it all the way up the system, step by step, to get anything done about it (see *How to make a complaint*, page 60).

The system can be very slow, cumbersome and inefficient. This may be because people follow the rules very carefully, but it could also be a deliberate way of putting off decisions.

A commonly-used method of putting off decisions that nobody wants to make is to appoint a select committee or sub-committee to study the issue in detail. The study itself will take time, and even when it's finished, the sub-committee's recommendations will have to be discussed by the main committee. But meanwhile the main committee can say it's taken action – by appointing a sub-committee.

If you don't think the system is working properly, or if it becomes obvious that your complaints or suggestions are being deliberately shelved, you can go outside the system and apply pressure in various other ways (see *Go to the authorities*, page 62).

Whether you keep within the system or go outside it, it's very important to prepare your case well. Discuss it with other people, in the school council, etc. (see *How to have influence*, page 49).

An efficient education system?

A Department of Education and Science circular has told all LEAs that there should be a maximum of 40 pupils per class in primary schools[199] and 30 per class in secondary schools. Few teachers and educationalists accept that these numbers are reasonable – but even these maximum numbers aren't achieved in most places. In 1964, nearly 18 percent of children in primary schools were

---

199 For many years the maximum class size in primary schools was 30, but this has recently been relaxed.

being taught in classes of more than 40, and 52% of secondary school students were being taught in classes of over 30. Since then the situation has got worse, not better.

Recently the amount of money for paying teachers and for new school buildings has been either reduced or not increased enough to keep up with the rise in population. Britain usually spends less on all forms of education than it does on defence.[200]

In 1966 the DES admitted that 2 million children were being taught in schools that were officially classified as "sub-standard" – i.e. nearly 25 percent of the total number of children at school.[201]

A recent survey showed that 25 percent of all school-leavers are virtually illiterate when they leave school,[202] and that 50 percent leave school with only a very rudimentary education. At a time when there are 600,000 people unemployed,[203]

---

200 Current figures show the UK spends about twice as much on education as it does on defence.

201 Ofsted, the body now responsible for monitoring school standards, estimates that 21 percent of schools are 'in need of improvement' or 'inadequate' which means 1.7 million children are affected.

202 This hasn't changed much in 40 years with similar numbers still leaving school illiterate and similar concerns about people leaving school with only a very basic education.

203 Latest figures show 2.24 million people unemployed.

there is a desperate shortage of skilled workers.

At the beginning of 1971, the DES admitted that we were 40,000 teachers short of the number needed to reduce classes to the recommended 40/30 level. No mention of course of actually reducing the maximum levels. It was estimated that the additional teachers needed would be found by 1975 – at which point the DES proposed to reduce the number of teachers being trained. It also mentioned the "encouraging" possibility of replacing teachers by machines.[204]

On the other hand there's an apparent contradiction. The DES say we are 40,000 teachers short, while thousands of teachers are out of work. Many of these are newly-qualified teachers just out of college, but some have been teaching for 15 or 20 years and then suddenly found themselves dismissed because the LEA is cutting down on the number of teachers. The DES says that the jobs do exist, but that teachers won't move to where the jobs are. To get a job at all a teacher may both have to move and accept

---

204 There are still no plans to replace teachers with machines but teacher shortages are still in the news. Another related issue is the use of non-professional staff to cover classes. Teaching Assistants (TAs) have been brought in since 1970 and their work is very valuable, but they are not intended to work as teachers.

teaching a subject he doesn't want to teach.
Teachers shouldn't be obliged to leave their home,
their families and their friends to find a job (nor
should anyone else).

About representation

School councils

A school council is a body which represents
pupils (and sometimes teachers as well). It is
the first step towards getting any school run
democratically.

Very few British schools have a school council,[205]
and very few of the ones that do exist have any
real power. Sweden is trying an experiment in
some state secondary schools where the pupils
can elect half the members on a "cooperation
council" which has real decision-making pwers.

A school council or similar body can be a very
good way of learning how democracy works or
doesn't work, even if the council can only make
recommendations and not decisions.

Do everything you can to set up a school council
in your school. Discuss the idea with friends and
sympathetic teachers. As soon as you've got a
reasonable number of people interested, call the
first meeting to get the council started. If you

---

205 Many do now.

can't get permission to use the school hall, hold the meeting in the playground if necessary – as long as you hold it somewhere. Use the school magazine, posters and notices, and word of mouth to make sure that everyone in the school knows about the meeting.

The first and all later meetings of the council should be open to all members of the school community, which means the cooks and gardeners and porters and caretakers as well as all pupils and any teachers and parents who are interested.

At the first meeting, you have to decide how the council is going to operate and elect the people you want to represent you. See *Working together*, page 81, for some points you should remember once you get the council started. It may help to get the council started properly if you can raise a problem that should be tackled immediately. But get the council properly organised: if you don't, it may just collapse once the first problem has been successfully tackled, and you'll have to start all over again.

If your school already has a school council, make sure it really represents your interests. The more people there are actively involved in it, the better and the more effective it will be.

Other representation

Teachers, parents and pupils ought to be properly represented on the board of governors of each school.[206] Instead, it's often difficult to even find out who the governors are, and there is no official channel of access to them.

It will probably be some years before this situation is changed. Campaign for representation anyway.

If you do manage to get represented, make sure your participation isn't misused. You may be made responsible for decisions over which you didn't have any influence, because you had no right to vote. Make it clear to your schoolmates where you stood. And demand of anyone representing you that they be careful about this too.

About democracy

If you want to have some say in the way things are done, to get things changed and to improve your own life at school, there are several things you should know.

Democracy is built on action. This doesn't mean unconsidered actions, but active contributions towards getting things changed.

206 Current rules say that school governors must be over 18 so it is therefore rare to find student representation on governing bodies, but teachers and parents are represented and governing bodies are accessible.

Democracy comes from below. You'll usually have to get a school council started yourselves. This doesn't mean you should refuse one if it's offered by the school. But unless there is sufficient will and activity behind the wish for change on the part of pupils, the school council won't function properly.

The method of organising should be suited to the problem. This means, for example, that the school council is usually only appropriate for solving problems which are faced by pupils from all years and classes. Problems which are only important to a certain group are sometimes better solved by a committee for just that group. Problems which only concern one particular teacher often need discussion and action only by his own pupils (see *Go to the teacher or the school council*, page 60).

About apathy

All changes require discussion first, to get agreement on your aims. All action must begin this way.

The most common argument against pupils' participation is that pupils themselves are apathetic and don't really want to be bothered about taking decisions.

The apathy may be real. This probably means that the problems aren't serious enough – yet. Things may be going relatively well. But the apathy may

214

be only apparent. It may be that pupils do feel dissatisfied, but can't yet express exactly what is wrong or precisely what they want instead. It may be because the headmaster or the authorities make it really difficult to participate in decisions – so difficult that pupils become frightened into indifference, or despair of changing things and give up.

If you haven't got a school council

Try to get one started. But meanwhile use other methods. Start working parties or groups to tackle specific problems, and dissolve them once discussion is under way or when the problem has been solved.

It's better to create a lot of working groups with limited aims than a few groups with big problems to tackle. Avoid having the same people in several groups.

Start with one or two working groups. When you have several (they should be created as problems arise) there may be a need for a coordination or communication group made up of one member from each working group, so that every group knows what the others are doing.

Make working groups open to anyone who wants to join, but make sure they don't become too big. Six to eight people is probably the maximum efficient number. If a group starts getting too big, it's best to divide the tasks up and create two groups. No task is too small to occupy a working group, but many tasks are too big for a single group to cope with.

Be receptive to your schoolmates' criticisms. You may think you're right, but remember, criticism is a sign of activity. Don't be put off if a lot of people criticise. Invite them to join the group and discuss their criticisms properly. This is an essential part of democratic life.

About solidarity

Another of the arguments against giving pupils the right to decide things is that they aren't "mature enough" and "can't see the real problems". People have said the same thing about Africans, Eskimos, Red Indians, Chinese, etc. You know yourselves what this argument is worth. But take care not to use it yourselves against younger fellow-pupils. Younger pupils often have different problems to yours. You should help them to create their own working groups.

Remember, too, not to be concerned only with your own problems. There may be other pupils or teachers who need your support.

A working group can help to get things moving if its actions cause discussion and activity to spread.

At some stage, when activity really grows and democracy is therefore starting to function, the need for a school council will become obvious and even irresistible. It may grow almost of its own accord out of the coordination or communication group mentioned above. Or you may decide to set it up properly at a formal mass meeting.

Differences of opinion and clashes of interest

It's normal for opinions to vary. Majority rule is a device for getting over this problem and keeping things going. The two main elements of majority rule are persuasion (getting people to agree) and voting (giving the majority power).

When people disagree, it's usually for two reasons: partly because they have different knowledge, partly because they find it difficult to understand each other. So the important things are to inform and to discuss. This is democracy. Some opinions are more right than others, some solutions are better than others. The important thing is to reach decisions based on adequate information and proper discussion. Democratic decisions are based on common knowledge and discussion.

But there may be real clashes of interest, in school as in society. Unlike differences of opinion, these cannot be solved by discussion. They can't even be resolved by methods of majority rule. They will almost always be about one group not wanting to give up power or share it with others.

In this case major actions and workers' struggles involving demonstrations, strikes or revolutions are needed to make democracy go on functioning.

Democracy doesn't mean only having proper information and discussion. There must also be the practical possibility of carrying out decisions. This last step is often the most difficult one, because this is when clashes of interest which may previously have been hidden come to light.

It's undemocratic to allow people to keep power if they use it to gain personal advantage or to prevent progress. It's democratic to take power away from such people.

School and society

Each school is a society. It's a small unit which leads an existence somewhat isolated from surrounding society. It's like a state within a state.

There are other similar closed societies – prisons, children's homes, borstals[207] and barracks, for example. Life in these institutions is governed by certain rules. Rules which seem quite out of step with the surrounding society.

In the surrounding society progress comes quite

---

207 Young Offenders Institutions.

rapidly. There is strong and active opposition to the authorities. Workers organise themselves in unions to protect their interests and to fight for change. In your society – school – everything is much slower.

School is nevertheless a mirror of our society. Society is built on economic power. This means that it's the people who have money and own industrial and commercial enterprises, here and abroad, who decide things. Just 5 percent of Britain's population owns 75 percent of its wealth.[208] 80 big firms own 63 percent of Britain's industry.[209] It's true that we can elect our politicians, but they can't decide anything which goes radically against the interests of big business. What you learn in school is geared to what society holds in store for you. You're taught to be able to meet the demands of this society. You're not meant to be interested in too much change.

The power and influence of big business is so strong that it affects the demands society makes

---

208 The inequality gap has been widening in Britain for some time. The top 5 percent in the UK hold 40 percent of its wealth whilst the bottom 50% hold 7 percent. See a video on wealth inequality in the USA here: www.youtube.com/watch?v=QPKKQnijnsM

209 This figure is difficult to verify these days due to globalisation and the relaxation of trade boundaries, but the point that large economic entities hold a lot of power is still true.

on schools. Schools change, many things are improved. But so far this has always been either because big business has needed the changes or because ordinary people have made themselves into mass organisations strong enough to force big business to give in to their demands for improvement. Our society is founded on the idea that people exist for the sake of big business – not the other way round.

Children haven't always had a right to free education. Up until 100 years ago, most children were treated virtually as slaves – cheap labour working in terrible conditions, down mines and elsewhere. Compulsory elementary education for all children, rich and poor, has only existed since 1876. Free secondary education for all children only became a reality with the Education Act of 1944. There are going to have to be many more long struggles before every child automatically gets the education he needs as an individual. Big business is not going to grant this right of its own accord.

Big business most clearly shows its interest in school in careers advice or vocational guidance. Vocational guidance and training are used by employers to tempt you in the right numbers into the jobs where they need your labour. Don't believe that the only career opportunities are the ones offered to you, or that you have to choose your career immediately you leave school (see *Careers advice* and *What can you do yourself*, pages 196 to 203).

Remember that once you've chosen a career, it's usually rather difficult to change later on in life.[210] There will be a much wider range of careers to choose from in the future than there is today. Don't take it for granted if someone tells you there's no future in the field that interests you most: this may just not be true. Don't accept that you can't become what you want to become just because you lack a particular qualification – there are often other ways of getting into a particular field.

Some people believe that school cannot really be changed until the whole of society is changed. They are right.

Others believe that society cannot be changed until school is changed. They have a point too. Society is made up of people, and it can only be changed by people. People are affected by what they know and what they are able to do. Everybody is affected by their years at school.

---

210 This is probably less true than it was 40 years ago. Many people can and do change career and the 'portfolio' career is a common concept, as is 'transferable skills'.

Many changes are taking place in schools these days. If they are changes in which you have played no part, you can be pretty certain that they aren't to your advantage. They are made so that people who have power can keep it.

Nearly all the changes in which you're allowed to participate are in things which aren't very important. The real and difficult changes are those which give more and more people power to decide more and more things for themselves.

Teachers and pupils ought to work together for change. There doesn't have to be conflict between them. In fact teachers have as little real power as pupils. They don't decide the content of their own education. They don't decide what to teach. And they decide very little about their own bad conditions of work.

Many people will tell you that changes are on the way and you only have to wait. But if you just wait you'll have to wait for ever.

Real changes to the advantage of both teacher and pupils should come from those personally involved. This may give rise to disagreements. Many will say that disagreements are bad. But that is only true of disagreements which have no purpose or aim. If you always try to explain your aim, many disagreements will be unnecessary.

Sometimes you have to fight against people who don't have much power, people who are afraid of change and afraid of having to make an effort themselves. This won't last long. In the long run teachers and pupils are on the same side in the struggle against the forces which control their lives.

You can't separate school from society. You have to change one to be able to improve the other. But don't let this put you off.

Every little thing you change in school may have results in society. Every little thing you change in society may have consequences in school.

Work for change always starts with you. The struggle is carried on by many different people in many different places. But it's the same struggle.

If you've enjoyed reading *The Little Red Schoolbook* and found it useful, please tell your friends about it. Pinter & Martin[211] is a very small publishing organisation and we can't afford to spend a lot of money on advertising. We'd prefer to spend any spare money there is on producing more copies of this book and other useful books.

---

211 Originally written about stage 1, but Pinter & Martin is also very small, with only three employees and a few trusted freelancers. See www.pinterandmartin.com/about-us for more details.